i

D

D040967

Building
Competitive
Immunity

A Strategic Approach
to Sales Success in the
Healthcare Marketplace

3 Chapters

Tom Stovall
and Dustin Grainger

Printed by Kirby Lithographic Company, Arlington Virginia

Editors: Karen Nelson and Laurie Stahl

ISBN: 978-0-9777745-0-0

Table of Contents

Profile of the Opportunity
Your Objective
Your Competition
Your Strategy
Tactics
Blocking, Trapping and Flanking
Resources

INTRODUCTION

CASE STUDY: THE DRAWBACKS OF PHASE II RELATIONSHIPS
CASE STUDY: NEW PRODUCT LAUNCH
CASE STUDY: FRIENDS AND RELATIONS
CASE STUDY: OVERCOMING OBSTACLES TO SUCCESS
EXERCISE: DEVELOPING A FRAG

Using Resources in the Field
Knowing Critical Success Factors
Building Positions on Reliable Resources
Driving Sales Performance Through Appropriate Incentives

Defeating Competitors Without Head to Head Attacks
Moving From Phase II to Phase III
Developing Phase I and Phase II Employees
Executing Competitive Positions

Knowing the Competition
Being Disciplined
Always Have a Plan
Understanding Sales Patterns

Dedication

A great amount of time (nights, weekends, and other personal time) went into the development and writing of this book. Needless to say, we know that the source of our personal focus and strategy is our kids, Lauren Stovall and Lily Grainger, who continue to be the inspiration for all that we do both personally and professionally. We dedicate this book to them. Thanks from Tom to Carol Stovall who was always available to serve as a sounding board for my questions and as a personal editor. Thanks also to Dick Stovall who generously shares with the SGI Team, the perspectives of a healthcare financial officer.

Foreword

A s a regional manager in the largest diagnostics company in the world I knew that our success as a team was dependent on solving our customer's most important issues. As a fighter pilot and trainer in the United States Air Force, I knew our team's success was based on tireless memorization of our capabilities as well as the capabilities of our competition. I also knew that the "fight" would be won by leveraging our unique strength against the vulnerable position of our competitor.

It wasn't until I sat through Building Competitive Immunity™ that I put the pieces together and it all made sense. After that BCI® session, I had the structure and template for use in developing "Phase III" salespeople. Most important of all, I now knew how to hire strategists. In today's healthcare environment, access to accounts will continue to decline for sales professionals who cannot affect their accounts' organizational strategy, or align their solutions to the critical success factors of the customer. If you're wondering how to learn that information at the account level, read this book, then hire Stovall-Grainger Inc. and you will not be disappointed.

As a retired fighter pilot and a former member of the Air Force Thunderbirds, I would have been unable to clearly articulate the Department of Defense's strategy for success when I left the service. Through the application of BCI and studying strategy as Stovall Grainger presents it, I can comfortably say the DOD's strategy has been a lethal mix of innovation and training. That combination continues to field the most potent fighting force on earth, however, against today's asymmetric threat of terrorism, it is a strategy that needs to be revisited.

How clearly can your sales and marketing teams see strategic advantage? How often do you hold "war games" to determine your winnable positions? Is your sales force "messaging" or positioning your product with its unique strength aligned to the customer's most pressing needs?

Consistently owning innovation in any category of business should always be a winning strategy, but what if your pipeline of innovation dries up? What if new demands for profit produce an R & D lapse, can you afford not to have strategists on your sales and marketing teams? Just imagine if your pipeline of innovation remains viable, how much you'll be able to outperform the competition with a "Phase III" approach by your sales force.

When I mentioned innovation as a key strategy in the DOD, I also mentioned training. I believe both are "winnable positions" for the US Armed Forces, but I also believe superior training is an insurance policy for a "competitive surprise" in innovation. You should look at your sales and marketing teams the same way. Regardless of where your business is in its cycle, adding strategists to your organization at every level is an insurance policy for your business. Whether you are launching a new product or defending hard earned market share, you won't find a better approach than Building Competitive Immunity™. I am such a believer in the process that I left my position as a VP of Sales in a healthcare organization to join Stovall-Grainger in November of 2006. Give us a call today, the competition is only going to get tougher.

Matt Modleski
Strategist and Fighter Pilot

Introduction

F ailure to understand healthcare issues from a broad perspective." In surveys we've done over the past ten years, customers consistently identify this as the main weakness of sales and marketing professionals. Not only do customers want sales professionals to be expert in their area of clinical focus, they want them to understand relevant issues at a higher level.

So what is this higher level something?

Strategy. Strategy is "that something" you rely on to meet your objectives and achieve your goals.

Technological advances and especially the Internet allow both the clinician and non-clinical influencer easy access to product features, benefits, core messages and technical performance information. "E-Details" and Key Opinion Leader testimonials are routinely included on company and product-specific websites. This is the new reality—in it customers are looking for something more from the sales call, something they cannot get anywhere else: expertise and guidance that only the sales professional can provide.

Personal interaction with customers is changing dramatically and sales professionals need to know how to change with it. Customers want to interact with professionals who demonstrate a larger understanding of their world and who can apply this perspective to topics relevant to their customer.

In today's marketplace, sales and marketing professionals must become more relevant resources for their customers. Doing so will gain them greater access to both current customers and to higher levels of influence in their accounts. This in turn will allow them to build immunity against their competition.

How does all this happen?

By being willing to stop using a purely tactical approach in sales and embrace strategy instead.

How do you get there?

The goal of this book is to show you this larger understanding always offers more opportunities for building a robust strategy. Chapters One through Five illustrate our approach to Building Competitive Immunity™ and teach you what the strategic process is and how to begin to use it. The remaining chapters introduce and apply the teachings of Sun Tzu's *The Art of War*. Understanding this classic and revered text on strategy will move you to an advanced level of positioning products and services strategically in the healthcare marketplace. Our intent is to be provocative in our more strategic, customer-relevant approach while also giving you ways to use it.

We would greatly enjoy hearing from you during your strategic journey. We are an email away if we can assist you as you develop more strategic, customer focused skills.

Tom Stovall and Dustin Grainger
www.sgbci.com

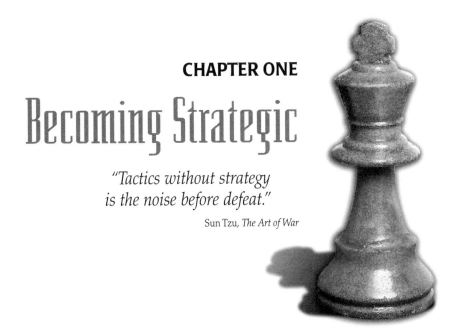

CHAPTER ONE

Becoming Strategic

*"Tactics without strategy
is the noise before defeat."*

Sun Tzu, *The Art of War*

Real breakthroughs come from exploring new ways of doing business. We know how difficult it is, however, to abandon old ideas, to move out of your comfort zone. But what if we showed you a way to gain a competitive advantage over your competitors that was more long-lasting and far-reaching than anything you are achieving now? A way that gained you greater access to your customers, provided a solid foundation for increased opportunities, and taught you how to fundamentally change your approach to your business?

As sales and marketing professionals, we need to become relevant resources to our customers. We need to gain access to our current customers and to higher levels of influence. We need to build immunity against our competitors in order to achieve greater professional success. To do all this, we must be willing to change—we must be willing to stop using a purely tactical approach in our selling and embrace strategy instead.

WHAT IS STRATEGY?

Let's define our terms. "Strategy" is a concept long shrouded in controversy and unnecessary mystique, with most eminent strategists disagreeing on a common way to define it. We define strategy very simply:

Strategy is "that something" you rely on to meet your objectives.
Tactics are the *methods* you use to meet your objectives. You cannot determine successful tactics until you have defined your strategy. While tactics are often described using
verbs, strategy statements almost always contain nouns. Remember, strategy is what
you *rely on*, not what you *do*. *What you rely on* and *what you do* together become components of your strategic plan.

Once you understand someone's strategy, his tactics make immediate sense. Let's look
at an example. To win the Tour de France, Lance Armstrong relied on a key uniqueness:
excellence in the mountains. He knew that, unlike most of his competitors, he didn't just
maintain his time in the mountains, he usually gained time as well—and passing his
opponents along the way gave him an additional psychological edge. *Excellence in the
mountains* was his strategy. Lance's training tactics, therefore, were aimed at supporting
his strategy. He bought a house in the mountains of Spain and started training there. He
slept in an oxygen deprivation "pup tent" to acclimate his body to the thinner air at alti-
tude. He trained more frequently on the actual mountain legs of the race than other rid-
ers. Everything he did—his tactics—supported what he was relying on—his strategy—
to meet his objective—winning the Tour de France.

Determining a successful strategy requires you know yourself, know your competition,
and know the terrain. Strategy requires constant reassessment: wins, losses, and
changes in terrain can all be catalysts for changing strategies.

There are many ways to use strategy. *Strategic thinking,* for example, is a current state of
mind that factors in probabilities, options, responses and potential outcomes and is an
immediate, "real time" discipline. *Strategic planning* is the process of engaging in the
same level of analysis in future focused segments such as three-, five-, or ten-year
strategic plans.

Strategic positioning is the science and art of discovering what can be relied upon to
achieve ones goals/objectives—in short, determining strategy. This book will explore the
discipline of strategic positioning.

Building Competitive Immunity

Finding a successful strategic position gives you key advantages over your competition.
Building your strategy on a strong foundation of critical knowledge—which we'll explore
in depth—and understanding of your customers' needs effectively "immunizes" you
against any *tactics* your competition might use. Because your tactical moves will be based
on a unique strategic approach, you give yourself an edge beyond your competitors.

But *how* do you build this Competitive Immunity?

Sun Tzu and *The Art of War*

We use Sun Tzu's *The Art of War* to illustrate and elaborate on strategy. Written approximately 2500 years ago, the book is a vital reference for anyone in a competitive situation.

The Art of War was written from an Eastern cultural perspective, which sees lessons learned as applying to all aspects of life. Significantly, this is how we approach strategy: your quest for Competitive Immunity must be an ongoing one, as it requires ongoing education, evaluation, adjustment and practice. Strategy in this context is very much a marriage of mathematics and art—factual analysis of your situation and then a more intuitive development of a relevant strategy and its accompanying tactics.

Let's look at an example of how a strategic approach succeeds where tactics without strategy fail.

Case Study: Strategic Positioning

I. The Situation

An account manager for a medical devices company had an objective to convert one of his key hospital accounts from an entrenched competitive product to his own company's solution. He faced several big obstacles:

- It was a highly competitive situation

- The competitor was well established in the account — to the extent that an important influencer refused to entertain any discussion concerning making a change

- Significant switching costs were involved for the hospital

- An important influencer put him off by saying they might be making a system-wide change in the future and it would be best to wait

This was, however, a major objective for the account manager and was equally important for his company. He could not afford to wait. What could he do? What strategy could be employed to meet this objective?

II. The Approach

A tactician would remain mired at this level without options. Unless his technology showed a substantial advantage over the competitor's, he would be reduced to either competing on price or waiting for this potential system-wide change—but without any indication he would be in a better position then to win the account.

Strategists take a different approach. They:

- Call higher up in the organization, allowing them to…

- Understand more globally financial and economic variables affecting the success of the organization, further opening the door for them to…

- Align their value proposition with those variables.

Our account manager took a strategic approach. He decided first to *elevate his level of contact* in the healthcare system to which the hospital belonged to get as clear an idea as possible of what was driving the organization. He also realized he needed to *gather more information about the terrain of* the account—the issues and business challenges the hospital was facing. In addition, he would see how he could *use his knowledge of a weakness in the competing product,* a weakness that might negatively affect quality of care to some patients.

Calling higher up in the organization meant approaching the Chief Medical Officer (CMO). Instead of making a sales call, the account manager's objective was to learn more about the professional and business performance challenges that were affecting the CMO and the entire system of care. Telling the CMO's assistant that he wanted only fifteen minutes to gain an understanding of the system's quality initiatives got him the appointment.

Prior to meeting with the CMO, the account manager did his homework: he read the system's website and did research on the Internet regarding their plans for the future and people in other senior positions. He found information regarding the CMO and his recent efforts to define and implement quality processes. This gave him some basic terrain information that would serve him well in his first contact with the CMO.

III. The Details

In his meeting with the CMO, the account manager began by saying he was not there to discuss his own company and products. Rather, his goal was to understand more about the quality initiatives within the CMO's system. He explained he would like to gain the CMO's perspective on those efforts, which would in turn help him look for ways his organization could affect those initiatives clinically and professionally. Having built some credibility with the CMO, the account manager was able to learn about two particular challenges that were being actively assessed within the system: both had to do with quality of care initiatives and current quality scores in specific service lines and with chronic needs patients.

Without ever getting into discussion about his company's products and solutions, the account manager was able to have an open conversation about the significance of the quality scores for patient care, for the system's competitive position, and for the system's current and future financial viability. The account manager also learned that if the quality scores continued low, there was a financial affect on directors within the system because a portion of the directors' bonuses was tied to measurable improvement in quality.

While the account manager began to see a solution, he realized it would cost the healthcare system both "hard dollars" (money spent acquiring the technology) and "soft dollars" (money spent for things like training the staff and switching patients to the competitive solution). To succeed, the account manager would have to address these economic and switching costs. The account manager also knew he would have to gather information from others within the account that might be able to "trump" the one influencer who was actively opposed to making the change.

Still following a strategic approach, the account manager again called higher up in the organization and asked the CMO for a recommendation. The CMO told him that he should meet with the two clinical department heads in the targeted service lines. The account manager asked the CMO to email or phone to help arrange short appointments with these influencers, as well as involving a colleague who covered the hospital where one was located.

IV. The Results

The account manager's move from a tactical to a more strategic approach so far entailed:

- Accessing higher levels of influence to both get around a stumbling block and to build his credibility and his case for switching from the current solution

- Calling higher up in the organization by asking for time to discuss critical needs, not to make a sales call

- Using resources he had at hand, such as the Internet, to gain information and credibility

- Asking those with whom he'd gained credibility to help him gain access to other high level influencers

- Involving members of his own team, who were able to assist because they understood what his focus was within the account and how they could support him with their talent and resources

This strategic approach gained the account manager critical terrain information about what important influencers felt was most important to their success and the success of the organization. This information in turn gave the account manager many more options with which to beat his competition.

This resulted in his being able to develop a specific strategy to meet his objective for this account. He came back to the organization with a solution—a strategy—that was:

- Aligned with the critical success factors he had uncovered

- Directly linked to the clinical weakness he had already known was inherent in the currently used solution

As a result, a pilot program was implemented employing his solution. Its success not only resulted in a significant contract with this key account, but it also was leveraged at other accounts across the country.

V. Summary: The Advantage of Strategy

The account manager's approach to develop a strong strategic position gave him Competitive Immunity, elevating him to a level where he could identify creative solutions and options and flank his competitors and, therefore, gain access to many more opportunities.

Relying on tactics alone keeps you stuck at a lower level, giving you very few options on which to compete. Strategy demands a larger view of the terrain, giving the strategist a bigger context in which to find different ways to position his products or services to align with the customer's higher level goals. Having these additional choices and variables almost always results in the ability to derive a winning strategy—especially if your competition has not taken the time to find this global context, thus continuing to strengthen your immunity to their tactics. In this case, presenting your product in this larger context will make the differences between you and your competitors even more pronounced than any position your company can create for you. And wouldn't that also make your job more fun?

BIGGER PICTURE CONTEXT: SEIZING THE OPPORTUNITY

"For those interested in developing more long-term relationships with our organization we suggest that they come around to our side of the table early on and learn about our business plans and our organizational strategies. They should be as conversant in the business of healthcare as they are in their areas of clinical interest. If they know these things up front, perhaps they can help us to begin to

develop creative ways to improve our clinical and business performance."

Integrated Health System Chief Financial Officer

A key requirement for achieving Competitive Immunity is to gain a bigger picture context. What do we mean by this? We mean that *sales and marketing professionals must have an in-depth and critical knowledge of the business of healthcare as well as their areas of clinical or technical interest.*

This is a major shift from what has gone before, a shift indicating a new paradigm for the healthcare industry, which is driven not only by traditional scientific and clinical variables but also, and to an increasing degree, by economic changes. The challenge facing most sales and marketing organizations is their ability to understand these changes from the perspective of their customers, to gain access to time and dialogue with key influencers, and to turn these new challenges into sales opportunities within the customer's environment. We'll be looking at how to overcome these challenges in this and subsequent chapters.

Crisis

The Chinese word for "crisis" is made up of two separate symbols: "danger" and "opportunity." Not one or the other, but both together. We are facing a crisis in how we sell our products, a crisis where there is, indeed, both danger and opportunity. Those sticking

with the old paradigm, unwilling to pursue a higher level of relationship with their customers, face danger as they are denied access and left behind as the market changes. Those embracing the new paradigm by taking a more strategic and consultative approach with their customers will find great opportunity, both professionally and personally.

How exactly do we seize this opportunity? Our healthcare customers say we need to do a better job of understanding their world. In a recent interview, a specialist associated with the Johns Hopkins Healthcare System in Baltimore told us that he would no longer meet with a representative for a social call—while also admitting he had a "select group" of sales professionals with whom he would meet at almost any time. He explained that they had earned this access through *their knowledge of the world of healthcare, not just their clinical expertise.*

One can say that this select group developed a bigger picture context via a thorough understanding of their terrain—the issues, trends, and business challenges facing healthcare providers. Developing a bigger picture context is part of a strategic approach. The tactical result of this work is that you will gain access where you could not before.

Gaining a Higher Level of Knowledge

Sales and marketing professionals usually have good knowledge of their own products and organization. They can also get fairly detailed information on competitive products and organizations from market research and internal and external sales databases. Unfortunately, this is knowledge readily available to everyone. What they often lack is knowledge that brings value to their customers—knowledge allowing them to bring creative solutions to meet customer challenges.

What do we mean by a higher level of knowledge?

A better understanding of key customers' clinical and economic realities will ensure that sales and marketing teams establish more symbiotic relationships with their customers. These relationships, in turn, will *enhance access to all levels of influence and to dialogue within the customers' organizations*. Depth and breadth of relevant knowledge will also enhance product positioning in a way that will increase your immunity to the competition.

Sales and marketing teams must be both more knowledgeable and more creative. Buyers are more sophisticated, more accountable and have less time to be "sold." For some customers, now is also a time of crisis—the complexities of their professional world transcend the old paradigm of clinical performance and now include challenging economic issues as well. These factors make buyers more demanding of the people with whom they do business. It is clear that to be successful, sales and marketing professionals must be able both to help buyers feel good about making sound clinical decisions and to help them justify their choices for clinical and business reasons.

How do you achieve this higher level of knowledge?

Begin to think in terms of what you know and what value your knowledge brings to your customers. We'll address the specifics of how you can do this in upcoming chapters, but for right now these questions will give you an idea of the scope and level of knowledge we're talking about:

- Can you articulate the current major challenges being faced by office and/or hospital-based doctors, nurses, service live managers, pharmacists, lab or radiology techs, and hospital administrators?

- If you asked a question regarding the key challenges facing my customer—such as the impact of recent trends in managed care—would you be sufficiently conversant with the subject to back up the question with credible knowledge and insight?

Out of these challenges and needs come your customers' Critical Success Factors. Critical Success Factors (Critical Success Factors) are imperatives that one must accomplish in the mid-term—generally within nine to twelve months—to achieve their desired goals for success. This mid-term time frame is critical. Focusing on shorter-term goals gives you little chance either to align your strategy to meet them or to thoroughly assist your customer in solving their challenges. Focusing on customer goals farther out than twelve months forces you to be too visionary and makes it difficult to provide concrete solutions to customer needs.

Providing Genuine Solutions

Remember the strategy of the account manager in our case study: he conducted terrain research, gained credibility and a bigger picture context, and looked beyond the "sales" call to provide a creative and genuine solution to his customers. By the way, a strategic approach to success is not unique to a hospital or health system environment. Office-based clinicians face similarly complex challenges and have higher level drivers that affect their clinical and economic decisions.

Healthcare providers are looking for these genuine solutions—solutions that help them meet their clinical and business or professional goals. To get to these solutions, we need to fully understand their challenges, which include issues like improving throughput, building employee satisfaction, and meeting measurable expectations for quality and service so we can provide solutions that integrate clinical and business performance challenges.

This means we need to acquire *healthcare business acumen*—a working knowledge of the business of healthcare. Healthcare business acumen gives one the terrain insights and this bigger picture context that allow for *more strategic and competitive positioning of products and services*. Those with the working knowledge of the healthcare business are the ones who will set the standards for performance in sales and marketing. Their customers seek them out and provide them with the opportunity to present their products and solutions because they see value in the knowledge and skill set they bring to the clinician.

By developing healthcare business acumen, you will understand the bigger picture of healthcare by including the other components of the healthcare "spend"—the component on which our key customers are placing increasing emphasis. This includes hard- and soft-dollar costs, quality, efficiency, and the "hassle factor"—the variables that impede the practice of clinical medicine.

It is important to note that healthcare business acumen has to be genuine. Just as there is clearly something missing when you see a six year old on TV singing about the pain of lost love, a lack of personal experience and understanding of high level healthcare issues will be obvious. Do the work you need to gain a thorough and personal understanding of your customers' challenges and concerns.

Where can you begin to get this knowledge? These basic terrain resources are a good beginning:

Resource	Description	Access
Wall Street Journal	Healthcare Edition: daily electronic newspaper focused exclusively on healthcare.	www.wsj.com Be sure to select the healthcare edition.
Modern Healthcare	Weekly print magazine and comprehensive website with archive search capabilities and daily email updates.	www.modernhealthcare.com
FDLI SmartBrief	Daily healthcare emails on business and policy trends.	www.smartbrief.com Be sure to sign up for the FDLI version.
Health Leaders	Daily healthcare emails on business and policy trends.	www.healthleaders.com

This understanding will allow you to begin to develop strategic positioning, build Competitive Immunity, and provide your customers with genuine solutions. You will understand how to integrate your product or service offering into the total business solutions of concern to the caregiver, whether a physician in independent practice, a laboratory or radiology director in a hospital, or a more complicated integrated delivery system. Your customers will thus see you as someone who understands their world and who shows them where your solutions fit and how they help meet their higher level needs.

Remember that strategy is "that something" you rely on to meet your objectives. Being able to rely on in-depth healthcare business knowledge will move you towards becoming a strategist and thus toward building Competitive Immunity.

Exercise: How Strategic Are You?

Strategists are constantly reminding themselves of their strengths, practicing how they will defend against their weaknesses, and keeping their competitors off balance. How strategic are you right now? Take a few minutes to fill out the following worksheet. It's okay if you don't yet have the answers. This is meant to show you what you need to understand about yourself, your competition, your terrain and your tactics. What you don't yet know we'll show you in the upcoming chapters.

1. *Strategists are always looking for new competitive space to stake out.* They believe that creating the future is more challenging than playing catch-up, and it is also much more rewarding. New competitive space might include: an ability to demonstrate measurable impact on a hospital's ability to improve efficiencies and thus the profitability of a particular service line; or an ability to reduce the "hassle factor"—the administrative challenges involved in using certain therapies or approaches to care; or, a measurable advantage (as defined by the customer) in clinical or technical performance that affects the overall continuum of care, not simply the episode of illness.

What new competitive space are you looking at right now?

_____

_____

2. *Strategists realize that imitating competitive methods is not going to create competitive advantage.* Strategists do not go into a customer meeting thinking that they have all the answers and just need to ask the right questions. Ways to move beyond your competition's practices and create competitive advantage include: moving from simply looking at yourself and the competition through your organizational lens.

What do you do now to create competitive advantage?

_____

_____

3. *Strategists develop a unique and independent point of view* about tomorrow's opportunities and how to position their products to meet those opportunities. This unique viewpoint and position might be.

List several of your own points of view about tomorrow's opportunities and how your product is positioned to meet them:

_____

_____

4. Strategists understand that it may be necessary to unlearn some of the old habits and practices that got them where they are today. They recognize that it is not enough to position one's products and services within today's markets. The challenge comes in peering into the uncertain future and developing insights concerning tomorrow's markets.

For example, perhaps you need to unlearn the practice of relying on basic product attributes such as dose frequency and recognize that in tomorrow's market, dose frequency is only a small part of the larger picture of highly specialized, highly potent, targeted therapeutics given in microgram doses whose advantages lie in their unique chemical attributes or in their unique dosage forms.

What practices do you feel you need to unlearn?

_____

_____

What changes do you see coming in your markets?

_____

_____

5. Strategists are constantly reminding themselves of their strengths and practicing how they will defend against their weaknesses.

Right now, what do you think are your main strengths?

_____

_____

What do you think are your weaknesses?

_____

_____

What can you do to defend against them?

_____

_____

Conclusion: Becoming Strategic

You should now have a better idea of what it means to be strategic. Remember: strategy is *"that something"* you rely on to meet your objectives. Tactics are the *methods* you use to meet your objectives. *What you rely on* and *what you do* together become components of your strategic plan. You cannot determine successful tactics until you have defined your strategy.

Determining a successful strategy requires you know yourself, know your competition, and know the terrain. Strategy also requires constant reassessment: wins, losses, and changes in terrain can all be catalysts for changing strategies.

In addition, becoming strategic requires an investment in knowledge: critical healthcare business acumen that allows you to understand better your customers' needs and concerns. Gaining this higher level of knowledge also allows you to provide creative solutions to your customers and to build a strong strategic foundation—in turn helping to build your Competitive Immunity.

Building Competitive Immunity requires you to:

- Realize that entrenched competitors are difficult to unseat and must be done so strategically

- Gather as much broad account and marketplace terrain information as possible well before developing strategy

- Understand that in order to gain access to higher-level influencers; you must first develop credibility through acquiring a bigger picture context—understanding your customers' global economic and clinical world

- Accept the new reality in healthcare: change is so rapid that an ongoing effort to remain current on important terrain issues and overall healthcare economic and business information is a critical piece of the strategic process

- Integrate both clinical and economic variables in strategy creation given the fact that customers' selection criteria now include both

Healthcare is in a time of crisis. Strategists will use this time to seize opportunity. In the next chapters, we will see how knowledge of self, other, and terrain helps us do exactly that.

CHAPTER TWO

Tool for Strategic Positioning

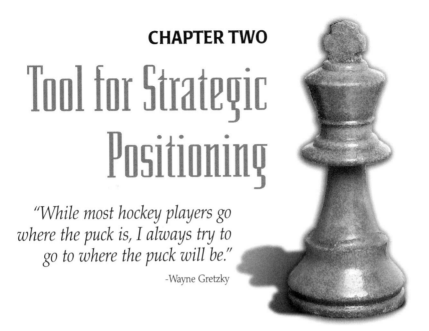

*"While most hockey players go
where the puck is, I always try to
go to where the puck will be."*

-Wayne Gretzky

Effective strategists always have their finger on the pulse of change, on where things are headed next. This allows them to take advantage—proactively—of emerging opportunities. It is impossible to always maintain a service, capability, or product leadership position—to stay ahead requires continued growth, and this requires the ability to reinvent one's products and services based on the changing needs of your customers. Strategists use this to their advantage, and are constantly looking for new solutions. They are willing, within the bounds of healthcare regulations, to consider possibilities far beyond the standard ways of doing business. They leave behind the danger of stagnation and embrace the opportunity of the new paradigm of strategic positioning.

PREREQUISITES OF STRATEGIC POSITIONING

Keeping abreast of your customers' needs to determine a successful strategy, however, requires that you know yourself, know your competition, and know your environment, both large and small. We've already begun to talk about gathering terrain knowledge. It is also critical, if you want to differentiate yourself, to embrace all three of these vital prerequisites of strategy:

- Know Yourself

- Know the Other

- Know the Terrain

Gathering and using information about yourself, other, and terrain allows you to identify a winning position that sets you apart from the competition—and that builds your Competitive Immunity.

Knowing Yourself

Knowing yourself encompasses much more than identifying your own personal strengths, although it is also important to be familiar with these. In this context, we define "self" as you, your company, *and* your products and services. In-depth knowledge of all these allows you to take advantage of your strengths and to minimize and be prepared to block for your weaknesses. You can also ensure you balance your and your product's strengths (and weaknesses) against your competition—and see how your product's strengths might address any existing terrain challenges.

Knowing the attributes, strengths and weaknesses of your products is fairly straightforward. To know your company, you need to be familiar with its financial resources, science, technology, and any other unique capabilities it brings to the table. Answering the following questions is a good starting point for gathering knowledge on all the aspects of yourself:

- What will you rely upon to win?
- Where are you willing to "fight"?
- List the core competencies of:
  - Your organization
  - Your product
  - Yourself
- What is unique about your product?
- What is unique about you?
- What position of your product or company cannot be defended against?

Questions you might want to ask about your own capabilities include:

- What am I passionate about?
- What is my formal education and training? What advantages does this give me?
- What is my Myers Briggs score? How does that way of thinking influence or help my selling?
- What unique capabilities set me apart from my competitors?

Knowing the Other

"If you only know yourself you only win 50 percent of your battles."

Sun Tzu

Assessing your competition is critical so that your end result is differentiation, not sameness. You need to know the strengths and weaknesses of those you are up against as well as you do your own—this knowledge will also help you know the larger industry and business you're involved in. Your customers certainly know your competitors. You need to know them even better.

Ask yourself these questions:

- Which of your competitors is the best performer in your market? Why?

- Who are the next three best?

- What are the potential future threats from other competitors not selected for either of those questions?

- Which competitor will scream the loudest if you achieve your main objective?

- Who is likely to attempt to displace you in each of your accounts?

- Where is the competition strong? Where are their weaknesses? Describe the "nightmare scenario" with your main competitor—what is the worst that could happen?

- Who supports your competitors in each of your accounts?

- What is the strategy of your competition? — *Do you know it. Do you know spies.*

Taking time to gather this information will help you identify your immediate and most important threats, and will also help you formulate your strategy as you work to become immune to the strengths, tactics and strategy of your competitors. Achieving immunity will also help prevent your "nightmare scenario" from ever happening.

It is important to note that strategists never lose sight of competitive moves but do not obsess over them. Responding to competitive moves without returning to your unique strategic position will not succeed—it is important to remain focused on your customer-relevant strategy and use that to lead you to success.

Knowing the Terrain

We have talked already about achieving a higher level of knowledge and healthcare business acumen. These are critical pieces of knowing the terrain. You need to understand the global economic and clinical variables that affect the success of your customers; the issues and business challenges that they care about. These will give you a specific context for developing a strategy addressing a customer's specific needs.

Let's go back to the case study in Chapter One. In order to provide a creative solution that would win him the business, our account manager worked hard to gather critical terrain information from sources at a higher level than usual to understand the underlying concerns and issues that might influence the customer's decisions. This is specific terrain knowledge about a specific customer—and our account manager made use of it by also ensuring he gathered more general terrain knowledge about healthcare issues overall, helping him understand the context of his customer's concerns.

As we've noted, gaining access to clinicians used to be easier. Today's environment is different. It's not just that access to clinical decision makers is growing more difficult—access to true dialogue, and to in-depth exchange of information, is even harder. Adding to the pressure are worried sales managers who are pushing their sales professionals to increase "share of voice" by increasing the number of calls they make.

Many sales professionals, intent on spending time with a targeted doctor or his clinical staff, bombard the doctor's office. Almost every conceivable method of seeing him has been explored, from lunches to "Thought Leader and Advisory Board" trips to sample closet organizers. Many of these doctor-rep encounters result in what we call the "bump-and-howdy" in the hallway—nothing much more than a brief greeting, a short, one-sided product pitch, and a signature for samples.

There is little value in this kind of interaction for either physician or representative. What does a valuable interaction look like? One physician told us:

"As a physician, there isn't much that I haven't already seen in my 20 years of practice. If I look at my typical day, only about 15 to 20 percent of my time is spent on the clinical side of the practice. The other 80 to 85 percent is spent on the business performance side of this enterprise. And to be honest, physicians aren't so good at that."

Sales professionals who develop a bigger picture context and who gather relevant knowledge of the terrain can make a sales call valuable for the physician (and, by extension, for themselves). Even the most difficult "no-see" physicians have certain sales professionals who get quality time. The secret to gaining access to time and dialogue is to be well-versed in both clinical and business factors relevant to the providers you call on. For example, in today's environment, Institute of Medicine reports, changes in third party payer reimbursements and various pay-for-quality measures are increasingly affecting the way physicians prescribe, the way technologists use equipment, and the way hospitals buy. A sales professional who can discuss the clinical and business ramifications of these developments increases the odds of gaining access to key customers and establishing symbiotic relationships with them.

Strategists tactically interpret clinical/technical information in ways that are more relevant to their customers—the way to do this is to know the terrain.

KNOWLEDGE EQUALS ACCESS

Clinicians are saying that salespeople need to shift from a pure clinical message to one that incorporates a more thorough knowledge of the clinician's professional and business challenges.

Acquiring and applying such knowledge—knowing the self, the other, and the terrain—is essential for earning more time with clinicians. Sales professionals with better customer access demonstrate a much more sophisticated and broader view of the business challenges their physicians, pharmacists, nurses, lab directors hospitals, managed care organizations, and other customers are facing. They regularly spend time studying trends on the business side of healthcare. They are aware of the current key success factors for their customers.

In Stephen Spielberg's 2002 movie, *The Minority Report*, we are introduced to a vision of the power of humanity and technology in the future. In the movie, advertisers target messages to individual consumers. Tom Cruise's character is seen walking through shopping malls as the stores and 3D advertisements call out to him by name and pitch their various products—but this idea of using information to target your message and win competitive advantage is far from new. In fact, if you are an Amazon.com customer, you have already experienced their ability to tailor their marketing messages to you based on your past purchases.

Successful product positioning depends on your ability to target your message to the specific needs of your customers and their organizations. In our conversations with physicians, pharmacists, hospital administrators, laboratory and radiology personnel, and purchasing agents, we hear a consistent theme when we ask how they would improve their relationships with sales professionals. They tell us that they need more specific information that is relevant to both their clinical and business performance objectives.

Ask yourself: *What would I say if a physician asked me about the affect the CMS changes in prospective in and outpatient payment systems initiatives on inpatient and outpatient use of my products? Do I know the top five business or professional issues for healthcare professionals?* If you aren't ready to answer, we encourage you to do some research into today's healthcare market. The resources we listed in Chapter One are a good starting point to gather this information.

Turning Knowledge Into Dialogue

"Information that comes far from the field of battle is essentially worthless; it will impoverish the strategist."

Sun Tzu

Your ability to gain and use targeted information to position yourself will lead to success. This means that you need to understand the specific challenges of your customers in order to position your products and services in ways that quickly grab their attention. The *quality* of your dialogue will yield more profitable sales than the *quantity* of calls you can make.

For example, how would you respond if you walked into a physician's office and the doctor asked you about your product's potential financial affect on his "at risk" patients? What if a pharmacist asked you to explain the differences or similarities you see between DRGs and APCs or the MSDRGs especially regarding your product's value in each? Could you answer? Could you easily articulate and position a value-added resource you have that could improve the efficiency of a provider's practice?

These are all real life examples of the dialogue level at which we have engaged your customers during recent field trips with sales representatives. You can do this as well. All it takes to raise the dialogue to a higher level is a bit of additional preparation. This will pay off: the result of this kind of dialogue is increased credibility and stronger relationships.

CREDIBLE DIALOGUE: THE STRATEGIC BUSINESS CALL

We admit that meeting the challenge of becoming more knowledgeable about your customer's world does require effort. It isn't something you can expect to download from some database or get handed to you by someone in the home office. The up-to-date knowledge you need comes from your taking time to investigate what is going on in your customers' worlds.

The Strategic Business Call process gives you the structure for doing this with your customers and with key influencers. We aren't talking about a *"questioning skills"* program. This is a unique process that shows you how to make a call in a powerful way.

Look at this as an ongoing process and *don't be afraid to ask questions.* Your customers don't expect you to have all the answers—they certainly don't have all the answers in their own practices. That's why they do a diagnosis before they prescribe.

Making the Strategic Business Call

The Strategic Business Call follows these steps:

1. *Why Am I Here? What am I Going to Do? Why Should the Customer Listen?*

Think about it. If you are seeking to uncover important issues faced by your customers it's going to be a different interaction than normal, right? The first step, then, is to make your customer aware that you don't want to engage in a technical or clinical discussion and that the reason for this call is different. Here's an example of how to present this: *"Today, Dr. X, I'd like to leave all of my product information in the bag. The purpose of this call is to gain a more thorough and clear understanding of the key issues facing you and your practice/organization. I'd like to ask you a few questions and take a few notes if you don't mind. I think that by having this discussion with you I will, at minimum, be more focused in the way that I can present products and services to you and the organization going forward and the more potential I have for identifying ways that we can impact your clinical and professional performance, Does this sound okay?"*

2. *Discuss Higher Level Healthcare Terrain Issues*

This step builds credibility and trust with your customer. Remember, your customer probably hasn't seen too many sales professionals taking this approach. Even after your customer has agreed to a different kind of discussion, it's important not to jump directly into "twenty questions" or too intrusive a line of questioning. Step Two, therefore, works to build trust. Here's an example of one approach you can take: *"I've been reading a great deal lately about Pay for Performance length of stay or capacity challenges, as well as managing financial and clinical risk at the provider level. What are you hearing from your peers across the country regarding these trends?"*

Take notes and listen actively during Step Two. You will be surprised to what degree your customer begins to open up. (A good overview of Active Listening can be found at: http://www.studygs.net/listening.htm)

3. *Discuss* This *Customer's Business*

You've now earned the right to drill down a bit and you can bring the healthcare terrain discussion to what we call the"neighborhood level"without being intrusive. This means asking the customer about issues specific to *her* practice or organization. Obviously, you need to do some homework on the local terrain before having this discussion. Here's an example of a Step Three approach: *"Before coming in today, I went to your website and was interested to learn about_____. That seems to be an interesting approach to _____. How is that going so far? How is your department/practice involved in these initiatives?"*

Additional ideas for questions can be found in the **Side Bar: Asking Intelligent Questions**.

4. *Uncover Customer Critical Success Factors and Key Goals*

You have now earned the right to get very focused and specific in your discovery. Critical Success Factors are items that are most important for your customer to accomplish in the mid-term in order to reach their goals. We generally define mid-term to mean nine to twelve months. Why not address long-term goals? If we uncover long-term goals, chances are that we won't be able to align with them within a meaningful period of time. When strategists uncover Critical Success Factors, they then seek to align their capabilities—either product attributes or service capabilities—with them and it is beneficial to do that quickly. Here's one example of how to uncover mid-term goals: *"Thanks for sharing with me your insights on these issues. As you look out over the next nine to twelve months, what would you say are two to three imperatives that you need to accomplish in order to be where you want to be professionally?"*

Equip Yourself for Dialogue

How can you best prepare yourself for the Strategic Business Call? By knowing the right topics and issues to address. With the evolution of healthcare comes a new paradigm for providers — based on clinical and financial outcomes. So, a customer's product recommendations—the buying criteria—are going to give significant weight to the financial side, with quality of care, patient satisfaction and improved efficiencies, and improved outcomes also all part of the equation.

Thus, the sales consultant with the greatest access to a customer's time and dialogue will be the one with a *balanced understanding of clinical and financial drivers*. She will spend just as much time studying the key business issues affecting her customers (perhaps by reading *Modern Healthcare* or *American Medical News*) as she does familiarizing herself with the clinical papers trumpeting her products.

In her reading and research, this higher-level sales strategist will look for new and creative ways to affect her customers' clinical and business performance. This will allow her to ask a broader range of questions that lead to a more thorough understanding of both the clinical and the financial challenges the customer is facing. For example, she might say something like, *"Doctor, I recently read a book about measuring quality of care at the condition level. I also know that this area of the country has experimented with several pay for performance models. From your perspective as a physician in the middle of all of this, how do you see your practice evolving to meet these changes and challenges?"*

Keep in mind that the examples provided above are just that. You need to find your own words to create a Strategic Business Call process that is genuine, sincere, and well grounded in relevant terrain knowledge. (Refer to the **Side Bar: Asking Intelligent Questions** for help getting started.) Once you do this, you are on the way to higher level dialogue and valuable terrain information.

Remember, we are facing a new paradigm. Salespeople resistant to change will question the need for having this kind of dialogue and will continue to focus on the quantity of calls rather than the quality, thus endangering their success. Those who are going to compete in the new healthcare arena will realize that they cannot do it *without* having this higher level of understanding and will embrace the new opportunity. Strategists, therefore, are able not only to position themselves and their products at a higher level, but they also "close the door"—build immunity—to competing salespeople because customers prefer the more consultative approach of salespeople equipped to weigh all the issues the customer cares about. Customers will allot more time to these interactions and give less (if any) time to those who take the traditional approach.

Asking Intelligent Questions

Strategists accomplish several things by engaging in higher level dialogue with their customers. At minimum, they enhance their credibility and differentiate themselves from the rest of the "herd of vendors." Ultimately, they discover opportunities to create a strategy to align their product capabilities and services with the terrain information they uncover and this is the real payoff.

Asking intelligent questions is often an effective way of differentiating yourself. Here are some questions you can use in dialogue with a provider working in a practice setting:

- What are the most significant business changes you've seen in your practice?

- There is a great deal in the press regarding employer coalitions such as the Leapfrog Group. How do you see this and other such

What goals do you have for your practice.

organizations affecting practices like yours?

- What are some things you're doing to improve quality while controlling costs?

- What is the inpatient/outpatient split in your practice? How has it changed in the past three to five years?

- How has the payer mix in your waiting room changed over the last five to seven years? From what to what

- What are the specific payer sources and methodologies in your practice? Fee-for-service, discounted fee-for-service, various types of risk contracting?

- Do you have a relationship with an integrated delivery system? If yes, what's the nature of the relationship? From your perspective, what are the advantages and challenges of these types of affiliations? If no, what other affiliations does your practice have? IPA? Any other assemblage of providers? Vertical relationships other than an IPA?

- What is your perspective on digital medicine and the Internet? Are you moving in the direction of a paperless practice? What do you see as the pros and cons?

- Do you have any "risk" relationships with payers? If yes, how are the relationships structured? What are the pros and cons?

- What training or professional assistance have you sought in order to make sound business decisions when negotiating risk relationships?

- Medicare, Medicaid, and other third-party payers are moving into pay for performance initiatives tied to quality measures. What are your thoughts on this?

Exercise: The Path to Access Through Dialogue

Begin to increase your ability to succeed in today's dynamic healthcare market by getting out of your comfort zone. Strengthen your ability to engage in meaningful dialogue by working through these exercises and ideas.

Exercises:

- Make a commitment of thirty minutes per week to learn about key issues transcending the immediate considerations influencing customers' day-to-day decisions. Refer to Chapter One for basic resources to jump-start this process.

- Seeking genuine dialogue with key customers will not detract from your call rate. Find an additional window of time each week to complete TWO higher level interactions.

- Do not confine your effort at meaningful dialogue to your clinical customers. Add at least one higher level interaction each with one of the following: administrative professionals, nurse practitioners, and

• When you speak with other physicians and providers, what are they saying are their most significant concerns regarding their practices?

• What trends to you see with regard to providers directly contracting with employer coalitions?

• If a business relocating to this area were looking for a primary care association for their employees, why would they pick your practice over any others in the area?

• What do you see with regard to the evolution of healthcare over the next five to ten years?

• With all of the challenges we have discussed as a context, what would you say are the two or three most important goals you have to achieve over the next year if you are going to be where you want to be professionally, and if your practice is going to continue to grow productively?

physician assistants. These customers are usually friendly and approachable, thus a great place to build your confidence in engaging in dialogue.

• After work, when you are with family and friends, do you talk with them the same way you talk with your customers? Do you use the same canned techniques to persuade them to see your point of view? Probably not. Think about how to adapt the approach you use with your family and friends to your conversations with customers — whose trust you also want. Practice this once during the week.

Points to Remember:

• Realize that moving from the "bump and howdy" to a level of in-depth dialogue will take time.

• Understand your customers will need to feel comfortable that you are sincere in seeking to gain additional insights into their clinical and economic or business performance issues. Dialogue is an earned right.

• Recognize that, in dialogue, you will not always know what answer your customer will give you. This is counter to the "needs selling" paradigm, in which probing questions are grounded in issues and challenges for which we already have solutions in the bag. In the Strategic Business Call process we are going through a discovery process, and this means we are exploring areas for which we may never have a solution.

• Unlike the outcome of the "bump and howdy" at the sample closet, dialogue is a continuum that builds over time. Solutions and quick remedies offered in a rapid-sequence, features-and-benefits pitch *foreclose* dialogue. Do not be quick to offer solutions; instead, seek a more thorough understanding before offering ideas.

Conclusion: Tools for Strategic Positioning

Strategic positioning has three key prerequisites:

- Knowledge of Self

- Knowledge of Other

- Knowledge of Terrain

Making time to gain a thorough understanding of each is critical for developing successful strategy. Terrain knowledge allows you to close the door to less skillful, tactical competitors because applying it raises the bar for what relevant and meaningful customer dialogue should look like.

Knowledge and information is the key to this credible dialogue and strategic differentiation. Information gains you access. This knowledge in turn puts you on the path to making a successful Strategic Business Call, following the four key steps of:

- Why am I here? What am I going to do? Why should the customer listen?

- Discuss higher level terrain issues

- Discuss this customer's business

- Uncover customer Critical Success Factors and key strategies

Success here relies on being able to ask focused business and clinical performance questions. Refer to the **Side Bar: Asking Intelligent Questions** for examples, and be sure you have done the appropriate terrain research to understand their context. This process will give you immunity to your competition.

Find 30 to 45 minutes each week to research your healthcare marketplace terrain. Make time for two higher level interactions each week. Practice higher level dialogue by also making time to meet with administrative professionals, nurse practitioners, and physician assistants.

CHAPTER THREE

Finding Your Strategic Position

"The essence of strategy is a positioning statement that sets you apart from the competition in ways that are important to the customer."

-George Day

hapters One and Two have provided you with important tools for strategic positioning: developing healthcare business acumen and a bigger picture context; gathering knowledge of self, other, and terrain; and putting these together to create a more strategic business call. All this information provides us with the material to find our best strategic positions.

STRATEGIC POSITIONS AND CREATIVE SOLUTIONS

Often, our strategy as we articulate it translates directly into a creative solution, or a strategic (winning) position, with our customers. For example, if an advantage of our product is that it reduces the length of stay or enhances service line efficiencies for hospital patients and we have a specific customer whose main concern is service line efficiencies and length of stay, then our strategy *is* our creative solution. In other instances, we must use the higher-level knowledge and context we've gained around our customers' issues to extrapolate creative solutions out of our strategic position. Armed with a solid strategy and relevant information, this is easily accomplished.

Building strategy on a strong foundation of higher-level terrain knowledge and an understanding of your customers' Critical Success Factors begins to immunize your competitive strategies. It still may be challenging, however, to differentiate your strategic approach to your customer. This chapter will examine how you can do that. Basing your tactical moves on a unique strategic approach will give you a critical edge over your competition.

What Strategic Positions Look Like

What do winning positions look like and how do you articulate them? Gathering and using information about yourself, other and terrain helps you identify what you can rely on that sets you apart from the competition. This can be expressed in a strategic, or winning, position.

This strategy, or strategic position, is not an action—strategy is a compelling position or attribute of your product or service and is usually expressed as a noun. The tactics that flow out of your strategy are the actions you will take to communicate your strategy to your customers.

Let's look at some familiar products and their winning strategic positions. Remember, strategy is what they rely upon to set them apart from the competition.

Product	Winning Strategy
Lance Armstrong	Excellence in the Mountains
Excedrin	Headache
McDonalds	Kids!
Venus Williams	Physical Power/Intimidation
Honda	Fuel Efficient Internal Combustion Engine
Cirque d'Soleil	Circus Reinvented

Strategy in the World of Healthcare

In our world, marketing teams give us a national brand strategy—attributes of our products we should use to sell them to our customers. How is what we're talking about here different?

National brand strategies are standard product positions that are well tested and validated and they do have value. These strategies are typically exclusive of any terrain considerations because they are created to appeal to the broadest possible audience: a once-a-day product has a clinical/compliance benefit over a more frequently dosed product regardless of whether you are in Memphis or Missoula.

Brand strategies might be defined as "gifts" with strong implementation requirements—sometimes they dovetail beautifully with your customers' needs, and at other times, you need to translate these strategies into a more relevant, targeted strategy addressing the more complex and specific needs your customers may have. Tactically, therefore, you must interpret these "gifts" to be relevant and specific to your customers and their terrain.

CRAFTING YOUR STRATEGIC POSITION

George Day from Wharton summed it up well when he said, "The essence of strategy is a positioning statement that sets you, your brand and/or your company apart from the competition in *ways that are important to the target customer.*" In other words, winning strategy is wrapped up in an offering to our customers that is meaningful and relevant to them. We can all remember product launches where we later found our customers not as excited about the product's strategy as we were—we need to remember that it is the *customer* who is most important during the formulation of a winning position.

Calling upon the development of your own healthcare business acumen is critical to formulating a strategic position that is important to your customers. What do you know about your customers' world—their clinical, professional and economic realities? In addition, what have you learned about yourself, your competition, and the terrain? Recall our account manager from Chapter One, who chose a strategic approach when he set out to gather critical information about his customer's challenges and needs as well as his competitor's weaknesses. This allowed him to present a solution that resonated and made sense to his customer—as well as meeting their biggest need, which may have been very different from the national strategy assigned to the product. Remember that the depth and breadth of your healthcare knowledge, as well as your customers' reality, will enhance the positioning of your product in a way that will increase your immunity to the competition.

Strategy is and always will be a controversial and sometimes confusing discipline. As we've noted previously, there are several ways to articulate strategy. It may be helpful to offer some "substitute phrases" for articulating strategy:

- What I rely upon to win

- My value proposition

- My unique offering
- My solution to an unmet need

Where can you go to begin to locate your own strategy?

Start With the Obvious

In our industry, it is often easiest to start with the obvious and look to the "big three" as a source of strategy:

- **Efficacy**: the most powerful strategy usually lives in a superior clinical performance story, if we have one to tell.

- **Safety**: Jack Trout, a respected author on strategy, says that winning strategy is often manifest in what our product or service *does not do*. In other words, are we a safer or more economic choice than what is currently on the market?

- **Convenience**: finally, are we more convenient? Do we appeal emotionally to an unmet need from a lifestyle or ease of use perspective?

A word of caution though: the "big three" are relatively benign without a tactical interpretation that creates relevance and value at the customer level. Every product is going to have a "story" around safety, efficacy and convenience—your challenge is to interpret these attributes in a way that becomes more relevant to your customer. For example, you can certainly argue that everything that emerges from the regulatory process has some level of efficacy—but what is *your* story? And how does that story impact practice efficiencies, length of stay, quality and patient satisfaction? Once you make that connection, you'll have a compelling strategy.

While each of these obvious advantages can be tailored to meet the specific needs of your customers' terrains, what if you can't find a strategic position within the "big three"? You then need to look further afield—a task made easier by your newly developed broader knowledge of healthcare issues affecting your customers. Here are some examples:

- **Economic Strategies:** if your product's clinical strategies are less compelling, you may be able to find an economic or fiscal strategy that fits. Does your product reduce Cost Per Case? Is there a managed care contracting strategy you can use that includes other products from your company in a performance-based arrangement that, ultimately, favors your specific brand? (While you can use unit pricing as a strategy, it is typically extremely limiting and not recommended.)

- **Packaging or Delivery System Strategies:** is your product packaged or delivered in a way that is advantageous to your customer? This approach may contain elements of convenience or economic strategies, or it may address very specific customer and terrain needs, patient population needs, or compliance issues. Examine your product. Does it come in vials versus ampules? A patch versus a pill? A convenience pack versus a bottle of pills?

- **Service and/or Relationship Strategies:** if your product is not providing a clear position on which you can rely to distinguish it from your competitors, look at your relationship with your customers and what services you may be able to provide them that set you apart. Can you offer them Continuing Medical Education? Thought Leader development?

While none of these alternatives may be as strong or lucrative as a compelling "big three" story, they do provide viable strategic positions and our examples will give you ideas of how to approach positioning your product and service. Using the tools outlined in Chapters One and Two—increasing and broadening your healthcare knowledge and gathering as much information as you can on yourself, your competition, and your customer's terrain—is critical to your being able to identify less obvious strategic positions and to your being able to articulate the most relevant strategic position possible. Remember that we are in a new healthcare paradigm, where access to customers depends largely on your understanding of their realities. Thus, the information and knowledge you collect translate directly into your ability to build competitive immunity.

On the next page are some examples of winning positions based on the new healthcare paradigm and the current concerns of our customers:

Exercise: Your Product Strategy

Now it's your turn. Using all the tools we've given you thus far, construct a winning strategy for three of your products or technologies. For each one, you should be able to come up with a list of options for a winning strategy. Fill these in on the next page.

Exercise: Changing Your Strategy

While continuity is an important part of a successful strategy, there are times that you will be required to change it and come up with a new winning position. There are only three conditions that might have an impact on the "lifetime" of a particular strategy:

- **Winning:** your current strategy might be a winning one, but what if you see a new strategy that promises to give you an even stronger edge over your competition? Subway did this when they adopted their new strategy of "health/weight loss." Their market share was strong but they took advantage of a trend they gambled would increase their success.

- **Losing:** Apple Computer went through several different strategies—including

The New Paradigm	Impact on Your Business Strategy: Examples of Strategic Positions
Managing Clinical and Economic Risk	Your product produces better compliance in blood glucose testing. Clinicians treating diabetic patients know better compliance reduces risk through tighter glycemic control, fewer complications, better outcomes. Your strategy should correlate your product's benefit to this reduced clinical and economic risk.
Quality and Patient Satisfaction: Pay for Performance (P4P)	Products that improve clinician performance or patient satisfaction should have strategies linked to these improved outcomes: • Fewer steps in the use process reduce the chance for medical error • Fewer side effects reduce levels of critical care and improve quality of care and patient satisfaction • If the product is part of evidence-based medical protocol then the protocol aligns with P4P
Profitability	At both a practice and hospital level, products that improve profitability can use this as a strategic position. Does your product allow for earlier discharge? Contribute to overall reduction in resource consumption? Provide system-wide or global use cost efficiency? If so, your strategy can address profitability issues even if your product is more expensive per unit.
Staffing Efficiencies	Hospitals and medical practices are facing severe staff limitations. Products and technologies that mitigate this issue can adopt it as part of their strategic position. If your product reduces or eliminates the need for intense retraining, or reduces the use of other products or process steps, then it improves staffing efficiency.

focusing on graphics, operating system ease of use and on the education market—trying to find a strong market position. None of their strategies were a match against Microsoft's widespread operating system and crushing market share. Apple turned its losing strategies around when they used their strengths—incredible product design, intuitive user interfaces, superior graphics capabilities—to develop a strategy and launch a line of portable information and entertainment products starting with the iPod.

Product/ Technology	Initial Strategy	Next Strategy	Next Strategy

- **Terrain Changes**: McDonald's original strategy of cheap, fast food homogenous in all markets could not keep them ahead of their competition when the terrain changed and their competitors offered customers the same convenience. McDonald's needed a new strategy to give them a major edge, and found it in their strategy of "kids." They preemptively and successfully changed their tactics to support their focus on children. Their evocative focus on this new strategy rejuvenated their competitive immunity.

Continuity and sustainability are critical attributes of a good strategic position and you should not consider changing your strategy unless absolutely necessary. That said, it is important to be prepared to both identify situations that pose threats to your current strategy and make sure you have considered your response in these circumstances.

Exercise: Staying Flexible

Identify for your own product what each of these situations might look like. Then, come up with circumstances that would force you to change the strategic position you developed above and propose one new strategy that would address the specific circumstances:

1. Winning: _____

2. Losing: _____

3. Terrain Changes: _____

SPEED, FAITH, AND THE HIGH GROUND

Now you have articulated a specific strategic position for your product. It's time to take it out into the real world of your competition.

When we work with organizations on product positioning and strategy, something quite disconcerting happens sometimes: seasoned sales professionals find they are unable to describe their winning positions compared to their key competitors.

In *The Killer Angels*, Michael Shaara's novel about the battle of Gettysburg, an English journalist asks James Longstreet, one of Robert E. Lee's most trusted strategists, what it takes to win. In the novel, Longstreet replies, "Speed, faith, and the high ground."There are key lessons to learn from this comment that will serve you well when your strategic position is up against a tough competitor.

Speed...

> *"Speed is the major factor in successful competitive action. You must take advantage of the situation before your competitor arrives. Exploit his lack of readiness. Attack his weakest spot."*
>
> -Sun Tzu

Sun Tzu says to win and win quickly.

This a principle we can easily apply to healthcare, a market in which competition is intense and where customers have become highly sensitive to acquisition cost. Physicians, hospitals, and your own organization are all looking for ways to improve their business performance. Therefore, it is imperative that you be able to identify and quickly achieve your top-priority business objectives, which you achieve by implementing your strategic position.

Speed and efficiency are essential in any competitive market. There are essentially only two *strategic* reasons for making a call on a customer. One is to learn the terrain; the other is to execute your strategy for the account (i.e., to position yourself and/or block your competition). Everything else is wasting your time and energy and that of your customers.

Note that, while we talk a great deal about understanding the terrain and while this is extremely important, we also caution against overdoing it. One of Colin Powell's 18 points on leadership is particularly relevant here: you sometimes have to make a decision with only 60 percent of the information you would like to have. Gather information on yourself, your competition and your terrain to the extent you need to, but understand too that in order to move ahead in a timely fashion, you must sometimes take the information you have collected to date and make the best decision you can, following what your intuition tells you is best. This will become easier over time as you do gain critical information. But in some instances, if you wait too long in hopes of getting additional information, you may miss your opportunity.

Faith...

Why do even the best performers sometimes become so frustrated? In some cases, it is because they do not believe that they can win. If you do not viscerally believe that you have at least one winning position then, when the going gets tough, you won't stay and fight.

When we believe at the organizational level that we have few or no winning positions, there is a tendency for us to cut prices. Before you do, it is important to remember:

1. Unless you are Wal-Mart, low cost is most likely *not* a sustainable competitive advantage.

2. If your customer tells you that they are going to take the lower-priced product, what they are really telling you is they see *no difference* between your product and the competitor's, between your company and the competitor's, or between you and your competitor.

Your job in this situation, then, is to redefine your strategic position to illustrate these differences for your customers so they see the value—beyond unit price—in your product over that of your competitor. Revisiting the four key steps of the Strategic Business Call in Chapter Two and the steps in this chapter on developing and testing your strategic position will give you the tools to do this.

We often conduct competitive analyses and war games for our clients. One of our central objectives in doing this is to come up with as many winning positions as possible. It's a very lively and compelling technique that involves looking both at your own winning positions and weaknesses and at your competitors' strengths and weaknesses all in the context of identified customer buying criteria, critical success factors, and strategies.

We had one instance in which a marketing team went through the war game without coming up with one single winning position for their product. We were astonished! We had been in the field with this company's sales professionals prior to the war game exercise and had identified winning positions after studying the terrain first-hand. To us, this was an indication that the marketing team felt themselves already defeated, a mindset that resulted in the loss of experienced, senior employees.

There is no reason for a situation to get to the point where such a devastating and costly solution is required. Your strategic positions are out there, they just need to be identified. Imagine a doctor walked up to you today and asked you to identify one place in her practice where you can provide a better solution. Working to get to where you can immediately answer this question will give you the faith in your position you need to beat your competition. Getting to this point will also create a proactive advantage for your team—you will not be fighting the competition but instead you will be immunizing yourself against them and their tactics.

"The General does not achieve excellence by winning 100 battles. The highest excellence is to subdue the competition without fighting at all. The key to victory is not in defeating the competitor but in defeating his strategy. For therein lies his vulnerability."

Sun Tzu

Faith is contagious: once you have put yourself in a position where you cannot be attacked you'll see a powerful rise in your team's level of confidence and motivation.

...And the High Ground

In business, the high ground is market leadership. If you had the leadership position and lost it, was it because you became complacent? We know that it is almost impossible to maintain a leadership position indefinitely, but it is always easier to defend a position when you hold the high ground.

Sun Tzu says to celebrate your wins...for one day. Then go out and explore the terrain, looking for high and low spots, boxed canyons, streams and rivers, weak and strong positions. You do this because, sooner or later, you will be attacked. Even modern day strategists align with Sun Tzu's premise. Cynthia Montgomery of Harvard Business School said, "Successful businesses can't afford to stop and celebrate their current advantages. They must be ever mindful of competitors and aggressively defend their position. This means continuous innovation, building new sources of advantages."

Thus, you want to build up positions of strength in your account and identify potential areas of weakness. Pay attention to anything that might be a sign of a competitive approach.

Remember that if you are fighting a strategic competitor, the competitor will not approach you directly. Instead, the competitor will work to flank you—winning a small foothold from which they will expand their advantage. They will also flank you by going to higher levels in the organization in order to gain access where you aren't, and to uncover organizational Critical Success Factors. You can defend against this by constantly communicating to your customer the value of your strategic position. As we have seen, if you connect your solution to your customer's strategy and Critical Success Factors, it will be very difficult for a competitor to unseat you. To help you do this, ask yourself these key questions:

- Are you able to recite from memory your current strategic positions?

- Is there any position you cannot defend against?

- Are you staying true to your strengths while being able to block your competitor's attacks?

Holding the high ground is a time of crisis—great danger and great opportunity. The opportunity is that if you stay focused on what you do best, it will be very difficult for a competitor to defeat you. The danger is in straying from this path to try and block your competitor's individual tactics. *Stay strategic*: strategists constantly remind themselves of their strengths, practice how they will defend against their weaknesses, and keep their competitors off balance by setting the buying criteria. If strategists find that they are not meeting their objectives, they revisit their strategy to determine if it needs updating As Winston Churchill said: "Strategy can be a wonderful thing, but now and then we must look at our results.".

Conclusion: Finding Your Strategic Position

Once you have gathered information about yourself, the competition, and the terrain and analyzed this in terms of your customer's specific needs and environment, you should develop a strategic positioning statement that clearly articulates your winning position.

In doing this, remember that strategy is what you rely on to achieve your objectives and that sets you apart from the competition. While your strategy may make use of the national brand strategy for your product, you may also need to adapt this national strategy to the more terrain-specific needs of your customers. And finally, you must be able to identify under what conditions you would need to change your strategy.

Taking your strategic position out into the real world requires you to consider how you will address your competition. It is important to know both your strategic positions and the healthcare issues of your customers well enough so that you can move and adapt quickly in the market; retain a strong faith in your position and convey that to your customers and your team; and connect your strategy to your customer's issues and needs rather than focusing on your competition's tactics. Set the buying criteria yourself by relying on your strategy.

Remember:

- Speed is a major factor in strategic success.

- You will never gain 100 percent of the terrain information you ideally would like to have. If you wait too long for information your strategic opportunity may be gone.

- A visceral connection to, and belief in, your strategy correlates with success. What you believe can be achieved strategically often becomes a self-fulfilling prophesy.

- Don't let possession of the high ground make you complacent—this is when you are most vulnerable to being flanked by a competitor.

- Proactively set buying criteria. As long as you can keep your competitor in a response mode, it is impossible for them to execute their own strategy.

In the next chapter we will talk about the three phases of strategic growth and how these relate to improved customer access and sales success. Specifically, we'll show you how the tools we've been discussing can be used to turn yourself into a Phase III sales professional—the most advanced level of growth—using the resources at your disposal to create strategic, winning positions.

Take the time now to fill out this personal skills assessment. In the next chapter, we'll show you how to work with it to pinpoint areas where you need to strengthen your strategic sales skills.

Exercise: Personal Skill Assessment

Use the following ratings to answer each question:

5: Highly Effective: I do this consistently, it is one of my real strengths
4: Effective: I do this most of the time and I can do it well if I make the effort
3: Fully Satisfactory: I do this sometimes, but need to be a lot more disciplined
2: Need Some Improvement: I do this on occasion, but need to work on it
1: Need Much Improvement: I rarely or never do this

1. Within an important hospital/practice/account, I develop multiple and diverse buyer relationships including those with individuals who may not directly influence our product's use within the account.	1 2 3 4 5
2. I understand the Critical Success Factors for each essential customer. (The two or three things they consider most important to their professional and business success.)	1 2 3 4 5
3. I plan a sales approach for each customer using materials that address his or her stated and unstated business and product needs.	1 2 3 4 5
4. I spend time during each sales call ensuring that the right steps are taken to expand my role as the customer's business partner. (i.e.. gaining information on business issues, discussing industry trends, etc.)	1 2 3 4 5
5. After each call, I assess how effectively I have advanced my sales strategy and make any tactical adjustments as needed.	1 2 3 4 5
6. I make it a habit to spend time learning about industry issues and how they are affecting our customers.	1 2 3 4 5
7. A part of my sales process involves understanding how a hospital/practice/account functions as a business, including who their customers and competition are.	1 2 3 4 5
8. In each of my major hospital/practice/accounts, I understand how customers shop, buy, use and dispose of our and our competitions' products, and I use this knowledge to differentiate myself.	1 2 3 4 5
9. In individual plans for each major account, I have outlined the steps for influencing the decision making process for getting new products into the hospital/practice/account.	1 2 3 4 5
10. I use knowledge of the political structure of each account to influence decisions in our favor.	1 2 3 4 5
11. I can tell you my major competitor in each opportunity and I can influence how important decision-makers differentiate our product from the competition's.	1 2 3 4 5
12. I take time to establish personal value with important customers that transcends the value of our product and company.	1 2 3 4 5
13. My customers seek my advice and input on business issues outside of our product specialty.	1 2 3 4 5

14. My customers offer information to me that is generally considered discretionary and available only to "insiders."	1 2 3 4 5
15. I am able to use account profile information to clearly communicate my sales strategy for individual products in each essential account.	1 2 3 4 5
16. After our product is purchased, I take time to leverage my success in order to further penetrate the account or increase product usage.	1 2 3 4 5
17. After the sale, I follow through to ensure that the product meets the needs and expectations of our customers.	1 2 3 4 5
18. The primary focus of my sales strategy and tactics is to build long-term customer partnerships.	1 2 3 4 5
19. I have a written plan for each hospital/practice/account that includes objectives, strategies, tactics, and resource needs for each important product opportunity within those hospital/practice/accounts.	1 2 3 4 5
20. I can identify and communicate the one factor of our product or service, which gives us the best chance to win in a competitive situation.	1 2 3 4 5
21. I am able to gain competitive knowledge in my accounts, which enables me to identify the best business opportunities for us and our customers.	1 2 3 4 5
22. My presentations go beyond specific product features and benefits, and include discussions of broader industry and business issues.	1 2 3 4 5
23. My customers generally allow me the time I need to accomplish all sales call objectives.	1 2 3 4 5
24. My essential customers view themselves as our allies. (They both like and respect us as business professionals.)	1 2 3 4 5
25. I am able to develop links between our organization and my customers', which result in mutually beneficial business gains.	1 2 3 4 5
26. I qualify all accounts based on the business impact we can have on them and the impact they can have on our territory strategies.	1 2 3 4 5
27. When I reach an understanding with customers, I can generally count on the customer's commitment.	1 2 3 4 5
28. I dedicate time each week to research issues, which may impact the business of each essential account and my individual customers.	1 2 3 4 5

CHAPTER FOUR

Strategic Growth— Breaking Your Narrative

"...Sometimes you have to break your own narrative to move forward...."

-Bruce Springsteen

W hat do strategic sales professionals look like in the real world? What pushes us to become strategic? How do we grow into our strategic potential?

We know the first requirement for Building Competitive Immunity is gaining a bigger picture context of your world and your customers. This means learning and it also means paying attention—paying attention to critical points where the terrain is changing, where there market is in crisis, and where we ourselves must change in order to survive. In the real world, then, strategic individuals possess a bigger picture perspective, see their world and customers in a larger context, and are comfortable with and positively oriented towards change.

Let's look again at the Chinese word for "crisis."

The Chinese word for "crisis" is made up of two separate symbols: "danger" and "opportunity." We know we are facing a potential crisis in how we sell our products. We have seen that those sticking with the old paradigm—being unwilling to embrace strategy and pursue a higher level of relationship with their customers—are in danger of being left behind as the market changes. Those embracing the new paradigm—by taking a more strategic and consultative approach with their customers—will find greater opportunity, both professionally and personally. The message is clear: real opportunity exists in being willing to change, move forward, and face the unknown.

WHY, WHEN AND HOW DO WE CHANGE?

"There are points in the life of every industry, organization, and individual where you must change dramatically to reach new levels of performance. If you miss these points, you will decline."

-Andrew Grove, Only the Paranoid Survive

Let's consider the opinions of several experts. Andrew Grove, former CEO and lead strategist of Intel Corporation, wrote *Only the Paranoid Survive* about the challenges of running a high-tech organization in the midst of the constant "white water" of change. Grove gives us a model for why change occurs.

Strategic Inflection Points

Grove speaks about *"strategic inflection points."* These are points in time when the environment changes so dramatically that reliance on the skills, behaviors, and practices that made us successful in one paradigm are no longer adequate. Grove argues that in order to continue to lead, to continue to be successful, we must be willing to reinvent ourselves—that to remain entrenched in the old way of doing business risks failure. As Bruce Springsteen puts it, we must break our own narrative to move forward.

Tom Stovall vividly recalls a personal strategic inflection point. "There was a time in my sales career as a hospital specialist that was clearly an inflection point. I was proud of my sales achievement. I had outstanding access to influencers, and I had developed strong relationships within the hospitals where I sold. I saw my sales on a path of consistent growth. Nevertheless, I remember sitting in my car, eating a sandwich as I looked across the Bay between Clearwater and Tampa, and thinking, 'this is the most boring job I could ever have. What more can I say about my products that I haven't said a hundred times?' I felt like taking the rest of the day off or at least driving to see some physicians along the beach."

Such moments of questioning are a normal part of growth. The *real* issue they bring up is, what can be learned from these moments that help us make it through the times of plateaued energy and performance? What pushes us to change?

The Growth Curve

George Ainsworth Land, another expert on the phenomenon of change, focuses on the growth phases of societies, organizations, and individuals. In his book, *Breakpoint and Beyond*, Land examines the requirements for success during a period of pronounced change. According to Land, when organizations find themselves stalling, they start to refocus on the basics. This reverting to basics, he argues, is a prescription for decline and potential failure.

Land tells us when and how change happens: change always runs in cycles or waves and the same cycles prevail in all types of growth, whether it is the growth of an organism, company, or civilization. There is always a period of chaos before a growth peak—followed by either rapid decline or further growth to a higher level than was previously thought possible, *depending on the path the organism chooses to follow.*

Land divides this growth into three stages:

- Phase I, the Formative phase: every system goes through this phase, characterized by exploration, basic learning, and testing limits. The system or person is seeking a successful pattern for living and further growth. Once a pattern is found that works, anything that doesn't fit into this pattern is discarded.

- Phase II, the Normative phase: in this phase, the organism or system repeats and builds on the pattern or system it devised in the Phase I. The organism sticks to the tried and true, where anything new is an extension of the old. This phase is typically productive and profitable but not usually creative.

- Phase III, the Integrative phase: if the system survives the disorder of the late Normative phase, it moves into Phase III where it is new, more creative and more mature. In this phase the organism operates outside of the old limits, outside the pattern. It takes a more holistic approach and finds its true potential through innovation and creativity.

Late in the Normative phase, the system's resources begin to be exhausted or markets begin to respond differently than they have previously. "Sameness" no longer works and the structure of the original pattern is challenged or demolished. Chaos leads to reordering and, if the organism is lucky, to the next higher level of order—Phase III.

To survive this disorder, this crisis, organisms must understand that the rules have changed. They must turn away from the old paradigm that is no longer successful and find opportunities in the chaos—they must reinvent themselves or else decline. Opportunity lies in this chance for reinvention.

Sales Analogies in the Three Phases of Growth

As Tom's example of his own strategic inflection point indicates, becoming bored and disinterested is a common late Phase II state of mind. This is where and when there is an opportunity to embrace a strategic position and move into being a Phase III sales professional.

The following table shows the various "sales states of mind" common with each phase of growth:

Phase I: Formative	Phase II: Normative	Phase III: Integrative
High motivation	Higher productivity	Creative
Excitement	Do what is proven	Innovative
Exploration	Benchmarking	Consultative
Basic learning	High trust	Big picture focused
Filling the day	Quality Programs	Solution-oriented
Not much productivity	Six Sigma	Strategic
	Consensus Driven	
	Even though productivity remains high, creativity wanes. One may become: bored, disinterested, plateaued, burned out, tactical	

Getting to Phase III is often born out of a crisis—embracing both danger and opportunity. The danger is how it feels to move outside proven limits, to look at doing things in new ways, to take risks. The opportunity lies in doing exactly that—the only path to growth is through taking these risks and stepping out of the familiar.

The *growth curve* below provides a guide, showing the three phases of growth that individuals, organizations, and entire industries go through. A strategic inflection point marks the beginning of each phase.

The Growth Curve:

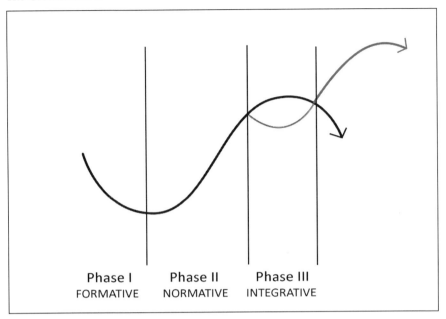

| Phase I | Phase II | Phase III |
| FORMATIVE | NORMATIVE | INTEGRATIVE |

With the Growth Curve as our foundation, we can look more closely at what's needed to achieve and maintain success as Phase III sales professionals.

Case Study: The Instant Photograph

Before we relate the Growth Curve to individual sales performance, let's look at a particularly striking industry example.

Photography has gone through an unmistakable inflection point. For over a century, the photographic negative was the only method for recording still photographs. Though significant improvement in films and emulsions occurred over the decades, most of the photographic industry was firmly built on film as the way for producing the end product Except for pros and serious amateurs, much of the process for developing and printing photographs was left to photographic labs. Changes occurred mainly in the realm of equipment but not in the actual photographic process.

Let's see how the three growth phases apply to photography.

In our example, Phase I of the growth process in the photo industry was a time for new cameras, lenses, film formats, and, in a few instances (notably, with Polaroid

Corporation) new ways of delivering the finished product. Photographic film, however, remained the unchallenged primary format for processing final products.

Polaroid arrived with a new idea for providing instant gratification—you could see your pictures in minutes rather than waiting a week or more. Typical of Phase I, Polaroid's first efforts were not the most elegant. In fact, early Polaroid photos were quite messy, unstable, and unpredictable. The company's idea was very exciting but lacking in polished execution and productivity.

As Kodak and Polaroid both moved into Phase II, they made their products and services more user-friendly as well as more technically stable and elegant. Polaroid enjoyed exclusivity in many markets. Kodak, though competing with other film manufacturers, achieved sustained growth by investing in film technology and steadily improving the quality of its products. Typical of Phase II, both companies were improving their products and processes based on what worked in the marketplace.

The strategic inflection point for the industry arrived in the form of digital photography. Digital photography offered a completely new method for delivering photographs, directly challenging the film negative that both Kodak and Polaroid relied upon for their success. This strategic inflection point was the crisis for these companies, where they could choose to reinvent themselves and embrace change or stick with the old paradigm and decline.

How could Kodak and Polaroid have misjudged the affect of digital photography? While both companies made moves into the digital arena—moves viewed as weak by knowledgeable observers—these were nowhere near the reinvention the crisis required, as both companies were heavily affected by digital competition, especially Polaroid, which was effectively flanked by digital photography as a new entry into the instant gratification snapshot market.

While Kodak and Polaroid floundered, organizations that embraced this new paradigm and took advantage of digital imaging, such as Nikon, Canon, and Sony (which had no role in photography in the film era), have been rewarded with significant growth.

The moral of this story is that Phase II organizations (and individuals), even if successful in the past, must realize that what made them successful previously may no longer be relevant in the new world of Phase III. These Phase II organizations (and individuals) must not only recognize strategic inflection points when they occur but understand them as clear indications that change will be required.

What often happens instead is that a kind of arrogance blinds us to the significance of changes that are underway. We may believe we know what it takes to succeed, but if we don't pay close attention to our customers and their industries we may find ourselves irrelevant in Phase III, still clinging to what worked in Phase II. We can discover that we're competing with organizations and individuals we thought we had long ago surpassed. When an inflection point hits, everyone goes back to zero. The playing field has been leveled. We must make a change or fail.

THE LEVELS OF SALES COMPETENCY

"Change and Innovation are vital to our organizations success as well as to the fulfillment of each member of our organization's team."

-Anita Roddick, Founder of The Body Shop

Because we are in the midst of a strategic inflection point for healthcare providers, we are also at a strategic inflection point for healthcare sales professionals. Let's consider how the three phases of growth look when applied to salespeople and the sales process. The table on the following page provides a summary of the sales competencies that characterize each of the three phases.

Phase I: The Formative Phase

Phase I, the beginning of *any* new experience, is a time of high energy, excitement, and motivation. For those (like Dusty) who received their first "brand new" car as part of their first sales position, the energy level during these early days of our career can be captured in one sentence: The "high" of the new car smell!

This is a time of exploration, learning, and building credibility. Perhaps you remember (or have seen) the focus of new, Phase I sales representatives. Their sales presentations are monologues. There is a fear that the customer might ask a question that they cannot answer. In this phase, we are still learning our way around our own products, organizations, and territories. Excitement and motivation are high, but solutions for customers are usually not very distinctive, and sales success is usually rather limited.

The Phase I representative's value to the customer is usually tied to explanations of product features and benefits. As the "sales states of mind" table indicates, a new person coming on board is not contributing as much to the organization during Phase I.

The Level of Sales Competency

	Phase I	Phase II	Phase III
Objective	Stay Busy	Hitting Numbers	Access
Sales strategy	Identify buying criteria	React to buying criteria	Set buying criteria
Calls On	Influencers	Users	Decision makers
Focus	Self/Products	Customers	Industry
Approaches Territory	Opportunistically	Tactically	Strategically
Planning goal	Manage time and territory	Develop accounts	Create partners
Planning focus	The sales call	The sales process	The end result
Time is spent	Making lots of calls	Developing accounts	Leveraging success
Call objectives	Present product	Identify problems	Create value
Presentations	Sell price/features	Sell cost/benefits	Sell value/benefits
Relationships	Casual	Trust	Symbiotic
Value	Product options	Problem solver	Strategic partner

Everyone goes through the Formative phase in his or her careers not once, but many times. Anytime there is a change in products, territory, or responsibility, the sales representative goes back in some way to Phase I. While this stage is usually short-lived, that depends on several factors, including how quickly one learns technical information and one's motivation, intellect, and prior experience.

Phase II: The Normative Phase

Looking at the Growth Curve, you see that Phase II is a time of upward movement—of sustained increase in sales success. It is a tactical phase—we learn how to replicate and streamline the tactics that work. Success is realized through becoming more and more efficient in doing the same things over and over again. Phase II sales professionals bolster the product knowledge they learned in Phase I and integrate a more thorough understanding of their customer's clinical world with their product and competitive knowledge.

Phase II sales professionals earn a level of trust with their customers that becomes a key contributor to sales success. They learn how to match their clinical solutions to specific patient needs, painting a picture of a situation where their product is the right solution. They are comfortable enough with their product knowledge that they invite discussion with their customers.

In the early part of Phase II, however, there remains a correlation between the number of sales calls and the degree of sales success. Phase II sales professionals still need to focus on the number of interactions they have with their customers. Phase II is a profitable time, but not always a creative time—especially when success and profitability have been achieved by performing repetitive tasks. This success can begin to plateau during mid to late Phase II as this repetition without creativity depletes energy and leads to boredom.

This phenomenon *always* suggests the need for some type of correction or intervention. After the initial stage of high energy we all experience in Phase I, many will switch companies to try and alleviate the sense of boredom only to realize that they face the same strategic inflection points with their new employer. The real challenge in Phase II is recognizing it as a time to reevaluate your career objectives or at least redefine what skill sets are necessary for your future success.

Most sales training is built on Phase I and Phase II skills and this was sufficient when healthcare providers were in their own Phase II worlds. We have seen, however, that healthcare is at a strategic inflection point, where there is significant change—under these circumstances, Phase III is where real success lies.

Phase III: The Integrative Phase

The Phase III approach to selling is strategic—built upon an expansion of the sales professional's base of information to include knowledge of the business of healthcare. It is a time of constant learning, and because of this the diminished energy experienced in

Phase II is not so much an issue. The importance of knowing the healthcare terrain in detail is irrefutable and this is where the Phase III strategist shines.

There is, however, a dip in the Growth Curve as one moves from the tactical approach of Phase II to the more strategic, terrain-oriented Phase III approach. Because Phase III sales professionals are on a learning curve, they need to direct some energy and resources toward understanding the world of healthcare, and this temporarily reduces sales results. As they learn new skills and approaches and gain higher-level access to time and dialogue with customers, however, the energy and motivation levels of Phase III sales professionals rise, pulling sales results up with them as they provide value to their customers that far exceeds their Phase I and II associates.

Phase III sales professionals are increasingly sought out by employers and by customers because the evolution in healthcare has spawned a need for this more focused—more strategic—approach to selling. While professional growth cannot be forced, one must realize that staying in Phase Phase I or II is never optimal for sales professionals, their organizations, or their customers. We only need to look at the abysmal access to Primary Care customers that the Phase II approach has created to realize the negative affect of the old, tactically based paradigm.

A Phase III approach incorporates key skills and understanding that overcomes many of the challenges endemic to Phase II and I.

THE STRATEGIST'S EDGE

"Theories and concepts are subject to obsolescence; brains and thought processes are not. In today's competitive marketplace, the mind of the strategist is an asset that always appreciates in value."

-Kenichi Ohmae, *The Mind of the Strategist*

Phase III sales professionals are motivated, effective, and worth their weight in gold.

So how does one advance to operating at the Phase III level of performance? You can start by looking at how Phase III sales professionals approach their business and their customers. A key differentiator from professionals in Phases I and II is that Phase III professionals use strategy and the strategic approaches we have been discussing thus far. They integrate a more thorough knowledge of their customer's professional challenges with their product and service solutions, allowing them to provide creative answers to their customers' most significant professional and clinical issues.

As strategists, Phase III sales professionals also have bigger picture knowledge of the healthcare industry. They are just as acquainted with magazines like *Medical Economics* and *Modern Healthcare* as they are with their company's clinical reprints, and they use this additional knowledge to differentiate themselves from their competitors. Since the healthcare industry is so dynamic, issues affecting customers today may be irrelevant to them in six months. By spending an additional 30 minutes each week reading healthcare business articles, you will greatly expand your knowledge of industry issues and improve your value and access to your customers. They will see you as someone who brings value to them beyond that of the typical salesperson.

By now you have a good understanding of what strategy is, how to identify your strategic position, when strategic inflection points force you to change or be left behind, and what attributes differentiate strategic, Phase III sales professionals. How then can you measure your own strategic growth? It is important for you to identify your areas of strategic strength so you can plan your continued development and know what you need to work on to build Competitive Immunity.

Self-Assessment

Go back to the self-assessment test you took at the end of Chapter Three. Your answers on this will help provide a graphic representation of your current perceptions of your strategic skill and behavior level.

Below you will find a table listing the four dimensions from the Skill Assessment Guide. Beneath each dimension are seven numbers that represent the component skills and behaviors for that dimension. These numbers represent the statements to which you responded in the exercise at the end of Chapter Three. Using your original answers, follow these steps:

1 Look at the number under each dimension heading and transfer the score you gave yourself (1, 2, 3, 4 or 5) for that number from your questionnaire to the table.

2 After you transfer the scores for each item number, add the total score for each dimension and place the total at the bottom of column.

Preparing & Planning	Gathering Information	Developing & Leveraging Relationships	Building Credibility
3_____	2_____	1_____	4_____
5_____	6_____	8_____	12_____
9_____	7_____	10_____	13_____
15_____	14_____	11_____	17_____
18_____	21_____	16_____	22_____
19_____	25_____	20_____	24_____
26_____	28_____	23_____	27_____
Total ____	Total_____	Total_____	Total_____

3 Take the Total Scores for each dimension above and, using the number scale on the left of the Personal Proficiency Analysis graph below, plot your score for each dimension on the graph.

Personal Proficiency Analysis:

This self assessment may be a bit biased as we do not get third party validation, however, an honest effort on your part can set the baseline for improving your strategic, customer-focused skills. You may also want to have your supervisor complete an assessment on you to gain additional insight. In general, scoring 4s and 5s suggest that you do well in that skill area, where 1s, 2s and 3s suggest that you could spend in these areas improving your skills.

Preparing and Planning – Gathering Information: These two areas are where people generally score lowest. Do not discount the importance of honing your skills here, however—information is key, and planning to win using viable and accurate terrain information is how you will achieve strategic success. As Sun Tzu said, "All battles are won in the temple rehearsal."

Personal Proficiency Analysis:

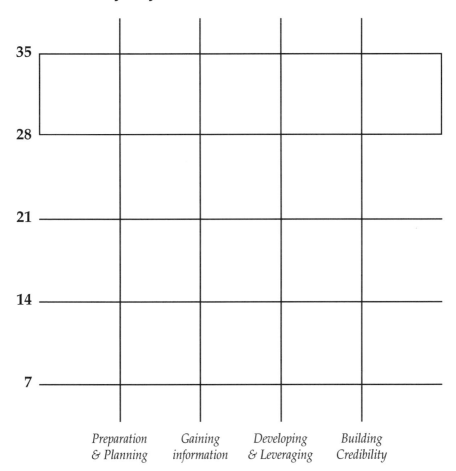

Developing and Leveraging Relationships – Building Credibility: Many of us believe that we posses higher level, Phase III strategic relationships already—but usually these are valuable and trusting Phase II relationships instead. It is important to assess very critically to what degree our relationships are grounded in true higher-level knowledge of customer Critical Success Factors and strategy. Make sure you are working to truly evolve your relationships to Phase III, and are not simply extending friendly connections.

The Skill Assessment Guide: Creating Your Phase III Skill Development Plan

Let's now take the results from your assessment and create an action plan. Please remember that there *are no right or wrong answers!* You simply score higher in some areas than in others. The guidelines above show you the importance of skills in each area—it is now up to you to put together an action plan to build up the skills in the areas where you are weaker than others.

Step One: Go back to the Skill Assessment Self-Assessment scoring worksheet and select one of your highest scoring areas and two areas where a lower score (1-3) suggests that you might want to improve your skills within each of the four categories. In the worksheet below, write in the specific Skills Assessment you were rated on.

Step Two: For the areas where you need improvement, ask yourself these questions:
- Why was I asked to rate myself on this—what is its importance to me and its relevance to my success?
- What one or two things can I do to improve myself in this area? Think back to the tools and resources we discussed in previous chapters.

Write down your improvement ideas. This forms the basis of your action plan—what you can work on in order to move you closer to becoming a Phase III sales professional—in each critical assessment area. Refer to chart on next page.

Phase III Account Worksheet
Now that you have identified general skills areas where you need improvement, you can also develop specific action plans to improve each of your account relationships. Remember, Phase III begins as a learning phase, and Phase III strategic and consultative relationships take a commitment of time and attention to develop, just as improving your strategic skills will take time.

The first step in formulating an action plan for a specific account is to ask yourself, what do you want your understanding of this account to look like **one calendar year from now?**

Use the questions on the following worksheet to focus what you want to achieve with this account. For each question, write down ideas you have for how you will achieve this higher-level understanding.

Account/Customer Name: _____

Skill Assessment Guide Questions	My Improvement Ideas
Preparing and Planning Skills Assessment Statement __ Skills Assessment Statement __	
Gathering Information Skills Assessment Statement __ Skills Assessment Statement __	
Developing and Leveraging Relationships Skills Assessment Statement __ Skills Assessment Statement __	
Building Credibility Skills Assessment Statement __ Skills Assessment Statement __	

What do I want my understanding on this account to be
one year from now with regard to:

Access? (Physical access to the account/customer *and* access to their mind)

How I Will Achieve it?

Understanding of specific customer/account Critical Success Factors?
(What does your customer need to feel they are succeeding and what
do you need to feel you are succeeding?)

How Will I Achieve it?

Understanding of the "Terrain?" (both immediate account terrain and
the larger industry terrain)

How Will I Achieve it?

Growing my company's and/or product's market share?

How Will I Achieve it?

Conclusion: Strategic Growth—Breaking Your Narrative

Growth occurs in predictable cycles, with the beginning of each cycle marked by a strategic inflection point—a crisis where systems and individuals are forced to adapt to the new paradigm or fail to thrive. Phase III marks the time of strategic, creative growth—and we are poised now at its opening.

Knowing we are at a strategic inflection point in healthcare right now, we also know that we need to change—we need to reinvent ourselves and become strategists in order to move into Phase III successfully. Using the tools we've given you so far—your knowledge of strategy, strategic positioning, and the strategic business call—will help you transform yourself into a Phase III sales professional. The worksheets in this chapter will pinpoint where you need to focus your attention and provide an action plan for your strategic growth.

Within the larger context of these growth cycles, however, are smaller cycles—so that strategic inflection points will always occur on some level in your professional and personal life. Remember that, when these critical junctions occur, moving forward is the often alarming but correct response. Going "back to basics" usually yields at best, what you've achieved before and usually, and poor results.

Use the worksheets in this chapter to chart your course into Phase III, identifying where you are already strong and where you need improvement. In Chapter Five, we will continue to consolidate these strategic principles and tools, showing you how to successfully handle difficult competitive situations and continue to build strong Competitive Immunity.

CHAPTER FIVE

Strategic Planning and Execution

"Strategy equals execution. All the great ideas and visions in the world are worthless if they can't be implemented rapidly and efficiently."

Colin Powell

I n the previous chapters, we've shown you what strategy is, how to define your own personal strategy, and how this can lead to increased access to customers, ways to address their most critical needs, and competitive immunity from your competitors.

We have also outlined the importance of being prepared to move forward as you—and the healthcare industry itself—reach strategic inflection points, reinventing your strategy to meet changing needs and opportunities. Once you incorporate these tools and this mindset into your everyday existence, you will be well positioned to build and preserve competitive advantage.

Putting all this together for each of your critical accounts can be challenging—there are assessments and analyses to be done, details to remember and consider, and individual strategies to develop for each account. Strategic planning can help you overcome this challenge. Preparing a strategic plan for your key accounts allows you to set objectives and execute strategy in a targeted way.

In this chapter, we'll show you how to do that as we review the key components of a strategic plan. We'll also test your readiness as a Phase III sales professional. It is important to keep in mind that, to be truly strategic, you must implement and execute what you know. You must act on the ideas for improvement you came up with in Chapter Four, bringing yourself to a higher level of understanding of your customer's needs and issues. You must put together a strategic plan that includes a competitive analysis, customer focused strategy, tactics, and resources against which you'll execute your unique strategy. And you must be prepared to act immediately in difficult competitive situations.

ARE YOU A PHASE III SALES PROFESSIONAL?

The tools we've given you and the Skill Assessment Guide you've completed have given you a roadmap of the path you need to follow to arrive at Phase III. Let's review the key attributes of a Phase III sales professional:

- They know their own strengths and weaknesses. They understand *what it is that makes their organization, their products and solutions, and themselves unique*, and they can explain this clearly and immediately.

- They know the strengths and weaknesses of their competition. They can handle their own weakness effectively when it is exposed, and by "taking the high road" they set a standard that undermines—fairly—their competition when misrepresentation occurs.

- They go beyond the expected knowledge of their therapeutic and clinical areas and become knowledgeable about the businesses of their customers.

- They understand what *each customer* believes is unique about his or her organization.

- They have dialogue with customers that leads to knowledge of the customer's clinical business and professional challenges, and they work to provide resources and product positions and solutions that address those challenges.

- They are keenly focused on strategy but highly agile with their tactics.

- Their interpersonal skills and marketing knowledge attract business and recommendations.

- Based on more thorough knowledge of self, other, and terrain, they can switch tactics and develop new approaches *faster than their competition*. Equally important, their customers allow them to do this.

- They understand that success depends most on people and ideas, and not simply on having the latest technology.

- They realize that fulfillment and empowerment come from creativity and initiative in their *current* positions. They don't need to rotate through other positions in their organizations to stay energized. This leads to increased productivity and lower turnover costs.

- They set the standard for communications. They understand what it takes to win, how to communicate this winning position, and how to make it happen quickly and efficiently. Others seek them out for their insights and their direction.

- Instead of being hamstrung by larger organizational issues, projects, and decrees, they are enhanced and empowered by the creation of lighter, smaller, and more mobile teams of sales professionals (Rapid Expeditionary Forces) who are given much more latitude to achieve objectives.

Why are strategic sales representatives in forward-thinking organizations given this greater latitude in how they do their jobs? Because they achieve their objectives quickly and provide excellent return on investment for the resources they use.

Test Your Readiness

Are you ready for higher-level dialogue with your customers? You are if you can answer this question:

What are the three key healthcare business or practice management issues facing your most important customers?

If you cannot answer, go back to your personal skills improvement ideas from Chapter Four. Following that roadmap will take you to the answers you need.

Phase III professionals are ready to move forward and evolve when challenged, rather than return to basics. This requires consistently looking ahead and making assumptions about the future. The following questions are the kind you need to ask—and answer— on a regular basis to be able to make grounded, strategic decisions to stay ahead of your competition:

- Which customers are we serving today? Which customers will we serve tomorrow?

- How do I access my customers today? How will I access my customer tomorrow?

- Who are our competitors today? Who will be our competitors tomorrow?

- What is the basis for my personal competitive advantage today? What will be my competitive advantage in the future?

- What skills or capabilities make me unique today? What unique skills and capabilities will I need in the future?

Proficiency in this kind of forward thinking is key to executing an effective strategy over the long term.

EFFECTIVE DIFFERENTIATION

"Competitive strategy is about being different. It means deliberately choosing a different set of activities to deliver a unique mix of value."

-Michael Porter, "What is Strategy?"

Michael Porter goes on to say that, "Strategic positioning means performing different activities from rivals or performing similar activities in different ways." Strategists are always looking for creative ways to position products and services, showing that they have a unique and higher value to the customer than what the competition is offering.

This kind of effective differentiation requires understanding of the healthcare terrain and a commitment to innovation. We do not necessarily need to invent something different. We do, however, need to help our customers address their Critical Success Factors with what we currently have in terms of resources, products and services.

Identifying Critical Success Factors

As we defined them in Chapter One, Critical Success Factors are imperatives that one must accomplish in the mid-term—generally within nine to twelve months—to achieve their desired goals for success. This mid-term time frame is critical. Focusing on short-er-term goals gives you little chance either to align your strategy to meet them or to thoroughly assist your customer in solving their challenges. Focusing on customer goals farther out than nine months forces you to be too visionary and makes it difficult to provide concrete solutions to customer needs.

Phase III sales professionals work diligently to identify their customers' Critical Success Factors. This, as we've seen, requires staying current on the changes in healthcare—something difficult for Phase I and II salespeople who tend to get immersed in day-to-day challenges. These success factors can change: if a physician group drops out of traditional healthcare insurance plans, for example, and markets themselves as a "concierge" practice, Phase III salespeople calling on the practice learn what the group sees as its new Critical Success Factors.

Obtaining information on your customer's Critical Success Factors and product selection criteria is a prerequisite for identifying winnable positions. Phase III salespeople know how their company's products are used and reimbursed by third-party payors, and are aware of any motivators or detractors to this product utilization. For example, now that Medicare and other third-party payers are rewarding physicians who practice "quality care," the strategic sales professional is entering into dialogue with providers concerning how their view of "quality" is changing and what that change means for their buying criteria. For a physician seeking to build her practice, meeting a payer's quality standards may mean that not only is she paid more for each covered life, but also that her practice is put in a higher tier, giving patients an incentive to use her services. The strategic sales representative will identify how his products and/or services can best integrate with the physician's goals for making the most of the opportunity opened up to her by the introduction of particular quality standards.

Case Study: Addressing Quality and Patient Satisfaction Criteria

A key customer has quality and patient satisfaction prominent on her radar screen, and the salesperson has validated these issues through higher-level dialogue with various professionals in the practice. To address these Critical Success Factors for this customer, the Phase III salesperson looks for product performance attributes that align with quality and patient satisfaction, such as: attributes addressing faster or better clinical outcomes, better or faster symptomatic relief, fewer ancillary tests or monitoring requirements, or a reduction in concomitant therapies.

The tactical professional might claim that these attributes are standard components of a core message. This can be true—but the difference is in how the Phase III strategist puts them to use. The strategic sales professional has taken the time to understand the most important issues of her customer and has selected key product attributes that directly address these issues, focusing only these key attributes and the message on the customer's concerns on quality and patient satisfaction. The remaining core product features and benefits are not used in this situation, as they won't resonate as deeply with this customer.

A valid question at this point is: "What if my product does not address my customer's key practice and treatment goals to any greater degree than the competition's"? There are two important considerations in this situation:

- Even if you feel your product does not address your customer's needs any better than the competition, being the *first to align* your product capabilities strategically with your customer's practice and treatment goals is *always* an advantage. Customers have choices and, in most technical and clinical categories, product differentiation is not always great. Being *first to align* can create, in and of itself, a strong competitive advantage. Remember, most sales professionals are tactical and are not taking these extra steps to make these strategic connections.

- Outside of product performance attributes, you may also achieve competitive advantage through service. Do you or can you provide data and information that specifically and uniquely assists your customers in achieving clinical and professional success? Are you positioning yourself as a resource that transcends basic information about your products and the standard educational resources that all vendors offer? Discover your customer's key information needs and meet them. You will achieve greater access and subsequent opportunity to position your products.

Phase III strategy is all about seeing the bigger picture—both the larger context of healthcare issues and the larger context of your own products and services. You must begin to think differently about how your products connect with your customer needs, seeing opportunities beyond the basic tactical approaches you may be used to. The work you are doing towards becoming a strategic Phase III sales professional is in many ways training yourself to think differently and to capture the lesson present in every interaction.

THE RAPID EXPEDITIONARY FORCE

It is clear that most healthcare professionals are limiting, or are preparing to limit, sales professionals' access to their time mainly because they don't see the value in the interaction. In most cases, this is a business decision based on efficiency needs. Healthcare professionals simply need more time and one way to free up time is to see salespeople less often.

As you know, we believe that physicians, pharmacists, nurses, lab and radiology specialists and other clinicians will *always* have time to meet with more informed representatives. These reps have the ability to achieve their objectives efficiently for both themselves and their customers. By demonstrating a higher level of understanding and relevance to their customers' world and their own organizations, and thus their value, they have often earned access to additional company and customer resources. Their customers welcome them without demanding the typical price of access (e.g., additional samples or free pizza).

There is an excellent military model for this type of sales professional and for a sales force made up of them, and it may be helpful for you to think of yourself in these terms. In speaking on strategy at the U.S. Air Force Air Staff and Command College and the Air War College, we learned about the value of the Rapid Expeditionary Force, or REF. The Air Force REF provides rapid, responsive, reliable airpower options that meet specific theater needs through a wide range of capabilities and it uses both to augment existing land-based forces and where a rapid response is needed.

The REF is a compelling concept within the U.S. armed forces, and its members perform at the highest level and are thus of great value to their organizations. Replacing the old paradigm of massive, slow-moving forces, the REF is a high performance, highly trained team that emphasizes personal development and responsibility over hardware. The REF model provides us with useful insights into what characterizes a successful Phase III sales professional in today's new paradigm of selling to healthcare providers.

Phase III strategists emphasize personal and professional development and customer and terrain analysis over their "hardware"—basic core product messages. They learn to respond quickly to changes in the terrain, to changes in customer needs, and to competitive attacks. They work efficiently, providing high value to customers without wasting their time. Their productivity and profitability are high and they are thus highly valued by their organizations. While your company policy may not spell out this kind of approach, don't wait until it does to adopt it or you will be left behind—if not by your company, then by your customers and competition.

Case Study: The REF Approach in Healthcare

The SGI organization conducted a strategy project with an orthopedic prosthetics company. The company was mired in a market segment that has, to a significant degree, become commoditized and driven very much by unit price, a situation presenting steep strategic challenges. Part of our orientation to the company and industry involved spending time in the field with sales professionals and actually scrubbing in for surgeries where their product was being used.

During one surgical procedure when the sales professional wasn't present, the orthopedic surgeon told us that the representative was ..."*as much a part of my surgical team as my scrub nurse and surgical P.A.*" Coming from an orthopedic surgeon, this was high praise indeed! When we asked why he felt that way, he went on to explain that, "*With all of my duties as a teacher and a private practicing physician, I know I should do a better job of keeping up on orthopedic practice management trends, regional payor trends impacting orthopedics and who in my marketplace is doing unique things in orthopedics. But I don't have to. She* [the sales professional] *makes me lazy! She knows more about these issues than anyone I know and she never fails to bring me relevant information on these trends. Don't get me wrong, she's always selling her products but she's also an orthopedic practice management expert.*"

It is important to remember this sales professional was seeking product utilization in a commodity category. Pricing in the category was essentially the same across all products, driven mostly by GPO competitive pricing processes. With level pricing and similar features across product lines, the orthopedic surgeon could base his product decision on issues beyond price. The sales professional in this case took strategic advantage of this situation, obtaining a clear understanding of this customer's Critical Success Factors and key interests, educating herself thoroughly on the issues in the industry and of interest to this surgeon, and thus creating unshakable value in the eyes of this specific customer. In fact, her in-depth knowledge and the value she created with this customer allows her to respond rapidly to any competitive challenge—she has effectively and thoroughly built Competitive Immunity in this account and is in a position to retain that regardless of changes in the terrain.

Relying on High Performance

"It will be difficult for you to succeed unless you look at things on a large scale."

-Samurai Miyamoto Musashi, *The Book of Five Rings*

The Phase III REFs rely heavily on high performance rather than hardware. This means looking at trends, looking towards the future, and looking beyond basic product messages. Healthcare professionals today are very concerned about the future, that the careers they laid out so carefully some years ago are now being dramatically changed. If you want to gain acceptance from these customers, you must understand how they are working within the changes they are experiencing—you must, as part of an REF, be able to respond rapidly and with a greater degree of understanding about your customers and their terrain. You must match your performance to the high level needs of your customers.

For example, a physician we spoke with recently told us about his transition from fee-for-service to increased risk-contracting. He said that the most important change he saw in his practice was a move from treating "episodes of illness" to "promoting wellness." This doctor went on to say that the way sales representatives could provide him with service was to discuss their products and services with him from this new perspective. He complained that reps were continuing to take the approach they were using 15 years ago when he started his practice.

The question you need to answer is how knowledge you gain of a customer's clinical, professional, and business issues will affect the way you serve up your core message and value-added services. When you can answer this question, you are on the way to a more focused and strategic level of dialogue with your customers.

Context and Confidence

Context and confidence will give you the credibility you must have in this focused dialogue. Strong awareness of **context** comes from having solid grounding in the subjects you are asking about. *The best test of context is your ability to comfortably answer the same questions from your perspective that you would ask your customer.*

Your working knowledge of key customer issues and your ability to discuss them in context will in turn give you the **confidence** you need. Our experience shows that the confidence and enthusiasm gained through understanding the healthcare business terrain is a force multiplier—a factor that dramatically increases the effectiveness of an individual or group.

You must be sure that you communicate your knowledge and understanding clearly, however. We have seen cases where the sales professional is knowledgeable but is not communicating his understanding very well. In other cases, the sales professional may appear uninterested because he does not reference important and relevant issues, or he does not open dialogue about these issues unless they are directly related to his clinical areas of focus and his company's treatment options. Shying away from areas key to the business performance of clinicians makes sales professionals seem narrow in their thinking, even if they aren't. This is why it is so important to identify issues key to your customers and to address them directly and proactively.

Ask your customers for their recommendations for sources of information for staying up-to-date on issues of importance to them. Read the journals they suggest. Get online and use Internet resources to gather information. All of this will help you gain greater understanding from your customers. Sometimes, just posing thoughtful questions to providers gains you credibility and, more importantly, the discussion following such questions will differentiate you from 97 percent of all other sales professionals. Engaging your customers this way will suggest new and creative ways of positioning your products and services that would not otherwise occur to you. You will also be treated to a new level of relationship and access that will give you a competitive advantage.

STRATEGIC PLANNING

Let's look again at Colin Powell's quote from the opening of this chapter: "Strategy equals execution. All the great ideas and visions in the world are worthless if they can't be implemented rapidly and efficiently." Handling multiple accounts strategically requires an effective way to prioritize and keep track of your strategies for each customer. Creating a strategic plan for each account is the best way to do this. We have looked at many useful tools for becoming a strategic Phase III sales professional but it is important to remember that at the heart of all of this is your unique strategy. The strategic plan is a vehicle allowing you to implement your strategy by organizing all the relevant information, analyses, tactics and resources.

No account, or opportunity, is exactly like any other. Typically, individuals and organizations draw up strategic plans for their major, or most called-upon, accounts, allowing them to outline and measure key achievements and ensure they approach these important customers as strategically as possible.

A solid Strategic Plan has six critical components we believe must be included: the profile of the opportunity, your objective, and an analysis of your competition, your strategy, tactics, and resources. Many of these will take us back to the first concepts we covered in this book—and are a good review for us as we look at each of these components in turn.

Profile of the Opportunity

This profile is, essentially, the executive summary or "state of the union" for your plan and is a valuable tool for understanding the key issues around each opportunity. It also describes the terrain of your account in detail—a key piece of formulating effective strategy.

- **General Information:** include here any overview information you feel is important about this customer.

- **Your History with the Account:** have you been successful with this account before? Or do you face significant challenges? Reviewing your history with this customer will help you identify competitive situations, possible tactics, strengths and weaknesses.

- **Competitive Situation:** who are your competitors? Be specific! The more details you include about your key competition, the more targeted you can make your strategy and tactics.

- **SWOT Analysis:** SWOT refers to your Strengths, Weaknesses, Opportunities, and Threats. By reviewing your history and competitive situation you should have a solid start on identifying all your SWOT components.

- **Account's Strategy:** what is your customer's strategy? In other words, what does this customer do to differentiate itself from other's in their local area? Why would a patient come to this practice when there are other options available?

- **Account's Critical Success Factors:** identify the Critical Success Factors your customer needs to achieve. Your plan should capture: Who you spoke to, when you spoke with them, what they identified as their Critical Success Factors. Helping them reach these goals will be a key piece of your strategic plan.

Your Objective

You need to formulate the specific objective you want to achieve for each account. You will use your strategy and tactics to reach this objective—thus, you need to follow specific guidelines when creating it. Objectives must be SMART:

- Specific: list exactly and in detail what you want to achieve.

- Measurable: how will you determine if you are meeting your objective or not? Your objective must be able to be measured.

- Attainable: Is your objective achievable?

- Realistic: Can you achieve your objective through the tactics and resources available to you?

- Time Bound: by when do you need to achieve this objective? Have you allowed yourself enough time or too much time?

Creating SMART objectives will help ensure your success in meeting them by requiring you to commit to a specific number at a particular point in time. .

Your Competition

Remember that a key component to becoming strategic is "Know the Other." Here you will include everything you know about your competitors. It is critical that you select specific competitors when you answer these questions; in order to build an effective strategic plan you need to have specific competitors in mind.

To determine your specific competitors and the attributes critical to your analysis, answer the following questions:

- Who will scream the loudest if you achieve your objective? If you are holding and protecting the high ground, who will scream the loudest if you don't allow them to take your market share?

- Who will try to displace you in this account?

- Where are they strong? Weak?

- What is the "nightmare scenario" with this competitor?

- Who supports your competitor in this account?

- What is your competitor's strategy?

Knowing your competition's strengths and weaknesses will help you see your own. Knowing your competitor's strategy will allow you to position yourself to the greatest advantage through your own strategy.

Your Strategy

Remember that strategy is that "something" you rely upon to meet your objectives. We have learned that determining a successful strategy requires you know yourself, know your competition, and know the terrain. We know that finding a successful strategic position gives you key advantages over your competition, and that building your strategy on a strong foundation of critical knowledge and understanding of your customers' needs effectively "immunizes" you against any *tactics* your competition might use. Because your tactical moves will be based on a unique strategic approach, you give yourself an edge beyond your competitors.

Strategy is:

• What you will rely on to win

• Where you are willing to take a stand

• A "core competency" of your organization

• What is unique about your product

• As Sun Tzu said, "A position that "cannot be defended against" by your competition

By using all the tools we have given you in Chapters One through Four, as well as the information we've asked you for in these strategic plan questions, you should be able to formulate an effective strategy for your most important accounts.

Tactics

We know that tactics are the *methods* you use to meet your objectives. You cannot determine successful tactics until you have defined your strategy. While tactics are often described using verbs, strategy statements almost always contain nouns. Tactics are *what you do*—strategy is *what you rely on*. *What you rely on* and *what you do* together become components of your strategic plan.

Tactics are the actions you must take to support your strategy and achieve your objective. All your tactics should have a date for execution and must either support your strategy or be used to block or trap your competition.

Blocking and Trapping

Blocking tactics are used to address legitimate and credible competitive statements and activities articulated by your competitors. Blocking allows you to address a competitor's moves against you proactively. You block their move in an attempt to neutralize or minimize the impact of their competitive move.

An excellent example of blocking came during Hillary Clinton's Senate campaign in New York. Her opponent was Rick Lazio, whose strategy was grounded in his statement, "I am a native New Yorker." Ms. Clinton blocked his strategy in their first debate. When she stepped up to the podium, the first words out of her mouth were "If your only criteria for voting in this election is that the candidate be a native New Yorker, then I won't get your vote. But I would like to address other issues that might also be important to you…" By doing this, she effectively rendered his strategy useless through blocking.

Trapping tactics are used when competitors misrepresent or mischaracterize your product capabilities or theirs. Trapping is the same as blocking with one caveat—you use a trapping blocking tactic only when a competitor is using misinformation. First you block, then you set the "trap" by making the client aware of the misinformation with a statement such as: "I promise that as long as I provide you goods/services, I will never cause you to make inappropriate or inaccurate decisions due to misinformation or incomplete information—I believe that if I did so it would damage my credibility with you now and in any future interactions. I'd ask that you hold my competition to the same standard."

Resources

Resources are those things, often beyond your immediate control, that are necessary to support your strategy and tactics and achieve your objective. Typically, resources fall into three categories:

- **Money**: you need financial resources to support your tactics, such as underwriting a Thought Leader session or budgeting for a small clinical trial or financing a publication.

- **Human**: you might find you need the expertise of people in your organization, such as experts in clinical affairs, managed markets, etc.

- **Time**: this is an often-overlooked factor in planning. Be realistic about the time you need to implement your strategic plan—to achieve optimal results, build in the appropriate time.

Think through your strategic plan, the tactics you've identified as crucial to achieving your objectives, and identify the specific resources you will need to execute your plan.

Conclusion: Strategic Planning and Execution

Phase III sales professionals possess a unique set of competencies, gained through rigorous and committed development of a strategic mindset as we've outlined in these chapters. These Phase III attributes will allow you to gain greater access to your customers primarily via higher-level dialogue. To ensure that you are ready and prepared for this, make sure you can answer readily the questions we've provided; these are also important to keep in mind on a consistent basis as you continue to move forward and adapt to terrain and market changes. You will base your individual account strategies on the conclusions you draw from continual assessment of yourself, your competition, your customers and the terrain—training yourself to be diligent and observant will pay off in increased competitive immunity.

Effective differentiation means finding new, different ways to position your products and services. A key component of this is identifying your customers' Critical Success Factors and then finding a strategy relevant to those needs. A useful model for envisioning the implementation of your strategy is the military's Rapid Expeditionary Force, which provides a rapid, reliable response to needs, terrain changes, and competitive attacks. The result of putting all of this together is the context and confidence you need to perform and succeed.

Strategic Planning is the tool you use to organize and implement all these essential elements of strategy. The six components of an effective strategic plan—profiling your opportunity, setting your objective, analyzing your competition, defining your strategy, outlining tactics and identifying resources—when brought together give you the most powerful way possible to build competitive immunity.

CHAPTER 6

Sales Strategy and "The Art of War"

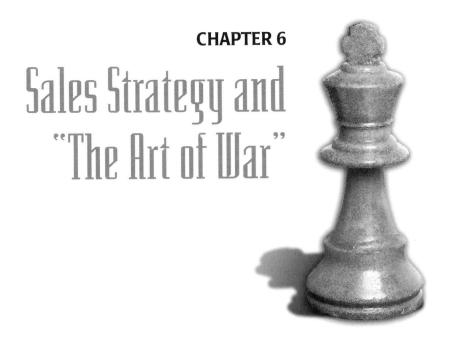

un Tzu's The Art of War is full of strategic concepts relevant to anyone in a competitive situation. Written over 2500 years ago during the Age of the Warring States in China, the book deals with fighting and winning a war—although Sun Tzu said that the greatest generals are those able to win without fighting. The book is thus as much about art as it is about war.

Eastern and Western cultures are very different in how they approach life. Western cultures tend to compartmentalize many of life's aspects and functions. Much like the departments within an organization, we have "functional silos" for the different areas of our life — religious, family, professional, personal, educational, etc. What we learn from one area of life seems to stay within that silo.

Eastern culture is quite different. Much credence is given to a holistic transference of lessons learned. Lessons learned through religion apply to politics. What is learned in personal endeavors applies to professional lives.

Using Sun Tzu's principles can address most of the challenges of strategic positioning in the healthcare marketplace and provide insights into how to be a Phase III sales professional. In the next thirteen chapters, we present Sun Tzu's text and our own commentary. While we have changed Sun Tzu's phrase "the enemy" to "the competition," we have kept our quotations current with Lionel Giles' 1910 translation.

Be patient as you read about spies, warfare, physical attacks, and deception in battle. It is important to read Sun Tzu's text as a metaphor for your current competitive situation—or, for that matter, any area of your life where you need to make choices and trade-offs in reaching a set objective. Try to see the deeper context of how strategy applies to all aspects of life. When you are able to make these connections, you will become much more skilled at facilitating, developing, communicating, and executing strategy. Strategy will become an intuitive process for you and you will be well on your way to increasing your effectiveness as a sales and marketing professional, and as an individual.

Our commentary will help you interpret his text in a more modern context and with relevance to the healthcare marketplace.

In the chapters that follow, Sun Tzu's text is in italics and our commentary on how Sun Tzu's principles apply to sales and marketing is not. Certainly, we have made no attempt to broaden our interpretation and application just to ensure that we "translated" all of Sun Tzu's work. Too many times we have read commentaries that are contrived because they purport to find a modern equivalent for everything Sun Tzu said so many centuries ago. *Our approach is leaner.* We have included the entire text, but we have not suggested an application for every one of the points Sun Tzu makes.

Please study the text and feel free to contact us with any questions you may have regarding our interpretation and application of Sun Tzu's teachings.

CHAPTER 7

Leadership and Information

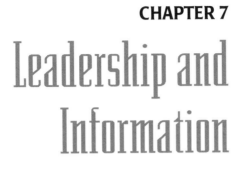

Sun Tzu said: The art of war is of vital importance to the State. It is a matter of life and death, a road either to safety or to ruin. Hence it is a subject of inquiry, which can on no account be neglected.

ales and marketing are of vital importance to the organization. Without effective sales and marketing strategy, your organization cannot survive. Historically, many organizations positioned their products in an environment with fewer competitors and a less enlightened customer base. Relationship selling and making lots of calls were often the keys to success—a tactical approach that traditional sales and marketing organizations typically relied on instead strategy. This tallies with Sun Tzu's approach to war and leadership—which is strategic, not tactical.

Case Study: The Drawbacks of Phase II Relationships

Tom Stovall recalls a situation from his own experience where he was making a call on a customer with whom he had a solid relationship. 'Harry, my main competitor in the therapeutic category I was dealing with, also had a strong relationship, and it was of longer duration. At the end of my clinical and technical presentation, the customer said: "Tom, if I use your product, what I am I going to do for Harry?"'

"I liked Harry too, but he was my competitor and I wanted to displace him in this account. Still, the customer was basing his product recommendation on his relationships with the salespeople calling on him. Harry had a longer relationship, and his product was an acceptable option, so this customer, concerned about the personal and professional affect on Harry if he used my product , was reluctant to switch. Since our products were similar, our relationships with the customer were our only real differentiator."

"Thinking about the situation for a bit, I came up with a solution for him. I asked him to recommend my product when I called on him, and switch to Harry's when Harry made the call. That was an acceptable solution for the customer. He was able to support both of us. The clinical decision was solid, and I was able to help him address his relationship concern."

The result of this tactical, Phase II approach was that Tom's only recourse was to call on this customer with greater frequency than his competitor. Had he spent time gathering pertinent information on self, other and the terrain, understanding the customer's key issues and how Tom's product and his competitor's product addressed those issues and solved this customer's challenges, he might have won the account's business outright. Today's more complicated buying criteria and more enlightened customers require approaches more strategic and more sophisticated in order to build Competitive Immunity against capable competitors.

Strategy is the key, along with the ability to understand your product, your competitor's product, and the customer's clinical and professional needs. Where better to gain this understanding than at the customer access point?

The art of war, then, is governed by five constant factors, to be taken into account in one's deliberations, when seeking to determine the conditions obtaining in the field. These are: (1) The Moral Law; (2) Heaven; (3) Earth; (4) The Commander; (5) Method and Discipline.

The Moral Law causes the people to be in complete accord with their ruler, so that they will follow him regardless of their lives, undismayed by any danger.

Heaven signifies night and day, cold and heat, times and seasons.

Earth comprises distances, great and small; danger and security; open ground and narrow passes; the chances of life and death.

The Commander stands for the virtues of wisdom, sincerity, benevolence, courage and strictness.

By method and discipline are to be understood the marshaling of the army in its proper subdivisions, the graduations of rank among the officers, the maintenance of roads by which supplies may reach the army, and the control of military expenditure.

These five factors should be familiar to every general: he who knows them will be victorious; he who knows them not will fail.

Sun Tzu also notes the importance of information. In his text you will see application of many sales and marketing concepts to leadership issues, but also his explanation of the "five constant factors" he notes above.

Historically, promotion to leadership positions in sales and marketing was directly related to success in selling. This has very little to do with strategic insight, however. Sun Tzu had little patience with leaders who did not understand the strategic process and how to develop and lead the troops.

Therefore, in your deliberations, when seeking to determine the military conditions, let them be made the basis of a comparison, in this wise:

(1) Which of the two sovereigns is imbued with the Moral law?

(2) Which of the two generals has most ability?

(3) With whom lie the advantages derived from Heaven and Earth?

(4) On which side is discipline most rigorously enforced?

(5) Which army is stronger?

(6) On which side are officers and men more highly trained?

(7) In which army is there the greater constancy both in reward and punishment?

By means of these seven considerations I can forecast victory or defeat.

The general that hearkens to my counsel and acts upon it will conquer: Let such a one be retained in command.

The general that hearkens not to my counsel nor acts upon it will suffer defeat: let such a one be dismissed.

Sun Tzu was highly critical of those who either did not understand strategy or who chose not to act strategically. This reflects a common concern we hear in our Building Competitive Immunity workshops—that managers will not support employees in this "new" approach to selling. We know that developing, communicating, and executing strategy is difficult. It requires that everyone in the organization be aligned in their approach and their expectations.

Sales and marketing leaders can assist their employees in developing strategic skills and outlooks by ensuring they do the following:

- Communicate clear expectations that support and reward strategic skills.

- Implement metrics to evaluate the level of strategic understanding of the sales and marketing organizations Identify and provide training for developmental needs to ensure strategic skills.

- Identify Phase III skills in potential new hires.

- Reinforce the application of the strategic process.

- Provide incentives for strategic, Phase III behavior to demonstrate your commitment to the strategic process.

- Plan for what you will do when you have a Phase II person where you need Phase III skills—have training and development programs in place to advance the skill levels of personnel when and where needed.

While heeding the profit of my counsel, avail yourself also of any helpful circumstances over and beyond the ordinary rules.

According as circumstances are favorable, one should modify one's plans.

All warfare is based on deception.

Hence, when able to attack, we must seem unable; when using our forces, we must seem inactive; when we are near, we must make the competitor believe we are far away; when far away, we must make him believe we are near.

Hold out baits to entice the competitor. Feign disorder, and crush him.

If he is secure at all points, be prepared for him. If he is in superior strength, evade him.

If your opponent is of choleric temper, seek to irritate him. Pretend to be weak, that he may grow arrogant.

If he is taking his ease, give him no rest. If his forces are united, separate them.

Attack him where he is unprepared, appear where you are not expected.

These military devices, leading to victory, must not be divulged beforehand.

Sun Tzu says, "All warfare is based on deception." In the sales and marketing context, deception has nothing to do with misrepresentation. It simply means that you should never divulge your true strategy to an individual who supports your competitor unless you want to lose—even when you call on the competitive supporters in your territory. Essentially, you need to know the terrain and the competition.

Of course, as sales professionals, we must remain always on the moral high ground. In this instance, however, we've seen that "deception" means taking care to safeguard your strategy. By knowing your terrain and the competition, you will know when your strategy can be revealed—and from whom you need to keep it protected. This knowledge of self, other and terrain allows you to use "deception" to your advantage. Here are three examples of how this can be done.

Case Study: New Product Launch

Once we were working closely with a sales and marketing organization that was preparing to launch a new product into a highly competitive market. Our job was to help ensure that all the sales and marketing people understood how to facilitate discussions around strategy, how to develop and test strategic positions through competitive wargaming, how to communicate the agreed strategy, and how to execute.

When we were deeply into the process, we were invited to look over the tools that would be handed out at a launch meeting that would occur two months prior to the launch date. Proudly, a member of upper management handed us a binder that completely captured the strategic process in six detailed modules: marketplace overview, objectives, the strengths and weaknesses of each key competitor, potential strategies, tactical tools and support, and resources.

We immediately recognized the danger of this approach—the managers were about to deliver their complete strategic plan to everyone in the sales and marketing organization. How many people in this meeting would still be around when the product was launched two months later, and how many copies of this strategic plan would be in the hands of competitors before the salespeople even began to execute? Needless to say, reason prevailed, and the binders did not show up at the initial meeting, at least not in their first iteration.

So what *can* you talk about? If you are going to disseminate any part of a product launch plan, make it vague enough so that when your competition gets their hands on it, they don't learn enough to focus their effort—or ensure it contains only obvious strategies and not the unique product attributes on which you intend to compete. You can, for example, wait to communicate potential strategies until very close to the launch date.

You can also feel very comfortable talking openly about the obvious differences in your solution compared to the competition. This allows your competitors to begin attacking these points—let them spend their time and energy fighting a battle that you *want* them to fight. When you are ready to launch your product, communicate your "real" strategies—the "real" differentiating points—to your managers so they can do the same with their teams.

Case Study: Friends and Relations

Here is another example of the importance of deception, or at least discretion: I (Tom) was working hard to establish my newest product in a tough, competitive area of my territory. One key influencer, who was very receptive to me and not so difficult to see, listened to my presentation and seemed to agree with my product's solution. But after several months of calling on him and presenting various aspects of my product each time, I continued to find that he just was not using my product. I was baffled. He agreed with what I said, he was very open with me, but he just wasn't buying.

Finally, I decided to be blunt. In my next call, I said, "Dr. Jones, for the past several months we have discussed my product and its use in your practice. You seem to agree with me that it's a valid solution for certain patients, but you haven't used it even once. Please tell me, what I have missed here?"

This prompted the doctor to tell me that his son-in-law worked for my key competitor. How could I have missed this? I knew my competitors, but I didn't know his daughter's husband was one of them. The doctor probably felt that if he supported my product, he would be taking food off his little girl's table. I knew I was never going to win. It would have been nice if I had done the work to uncover this problem six months earlier. All I could imagine were the points of discussion the doctor was having with his son-in-law at their regular Saturday evening visits. He probably told his son-in-law everything I said.

I continued to call on this doctor because he was a key influencer in therapeutic areas where his son-in-law was not a competitor. (But rest assured that I asked him if he had any other family members in the industry that I should know about. He thought that was humorous. I did not.) You should also know that I never gave away any more strategic information about my product that I didn't want getting back to his son-in-law. For example, I would ask the doctor to consider my product due to its dosing schedule or some other *non-essential* attribute. He never acquiesced, but I figured that at least his next discussion with his son-in-law could lead the son-in-law to spend time and energy defending his product versus mine in an area that was really off strategy for me. This was, in Sun Tzu's terms, using deception. The benefits in this case were that I continued to have a beneficial relationship with this customer without giving away my strategy and, perhaps, guide my competition to spend energy in areas that were not strategic for me. We have all had accounts like this "lost" one, where use of deception is a valid approach to keep the competitors off balance.

Case Study: Overcoming Obstacles to Success

As we've seen, it is very important to gain access to individuals at all levels of an account, which makes you less likely to be flanked by your competition. This will mean gaining access to people who may have a vested interest in keeping you from succeeding. These individuals could be part of decision teams, and giving them your strategy will allow them to better influence other members of the team against you.

When working with another client on an effort to convert a Group Purchasing Organization to their product solution, we ran into this situation. In this particular account, the National Account Manager had done his job. He had gotten into the buying cycle early, identified all the buying influences, and conducted strategic business calls with most of them. We had only one real concern regarding the decision makers. One of them had worked in the past for a competitive company that was also a player in this opportunity.

Part of "knowing the terrain" is having background information regarding an individual's professional experience. We asked the Account Manager to contact his ally within the account to see if he could shed some light on why the individual in question had left the competitive company. Was the parting amicable, or was there bad blood? If it turned out that the person's experience with his previous company was positive or neutral, our recommendation was to be very cautious with him and to follow Sun Tzu's advice: If you are going to approach a competitor who is heavily armed and dug in, you must have five-to-one superiority in order to have adequate potential to succeed. At this account, that would mean finding at least five other key individuals who would support the Account Manager's positioning of his product solution.

Clearly, it is critical to do the work required to know yourself, your competition and, in these instances, particularly your terrain. Having detailed terrain knowledge helps when you are deciding whether to communicate your strategy or, instead, to use tactical deception.

Now the general who wins a battle makes many calculations in his temple ere the battle is fought. The general who loses a battle makes but few calculations beforehand. Thus do many calculations lead to victory and few calculations to defeat: how much more no calculation at all. It is by attention to this point that I can foresee who is likely to win or lose.

Sun Tzu tells us here that nothing replaces preparation. We have just seen the importance of gathering and interpreting critical information—knowing yourself, the competition, the terrain—now, what can you do with all this to be as best prepared as possible?

Looking back at Chapters 1 through 5, let's consider what planning tools we can use:

- Knowing the steps of the Strategic Business Call

- Developing a Strategic Position based on strengths and knowledge

- Conducting regular Strategic Skills Assessments on yourself and noting areas needing improvement and putting together a self-improvement plan

- Identifying customer critical success factors and building these into a Strategic Plan

While we are all often in a hurry to get in front of our customers, Sun Tzu teaches that if we do not consider the situation prior to a competitive encounter, we are likely to suffer defeat. This is especially true when we are up against a competitor who either has a better relationship or is functioning at the Phase III level. It is critical to know two main pieces of information about our accounts:

- What are the critical success factors for the influencers in this account? In other words, for each individual, what are the issues and challenges that the individual feels must be addressed in the short term (9-12 months) in order for him or her to enjoy personal, professional, and organizational success?

- What is this account's own strategy? What do they believe differentiates them from their competitors, or, as we like to say, what are they relying on to win in their market?

Focusing on these two issues ensures that all your activity around your accounts will be based on your strategic position for that account. Do not shortchange your account planning process thinking it is not a valuable use of your time—if you are capturing the right information, your plan can be concise, easily communicated, and valuable for keeping you focused on what is most important for the particular account.

Exercise: Developing a Frag

In the military, there is something called a "frago," "frag," or "fragmentary." If a leader is in the field with his troops, he might walk up to the person responsible and deliver or ask them for a "frag." This is a focused, concise presentation of what is going on day to day in the field and what has happened that has required a change to a previous order. The "frag" doesn't contain everything that may be found in the initial order or plan, only the required changes that are affecting that day's activity.

We encourage you to adapt the concept of "fragmentary" to your strategic account planning. Your Account Fragmentary should be a one-page document that you carry with you for each of the accounts you will be visiting on a particular day. It is also what you provide to anyone who might be working with you during a field visit that day. You can use the Phase III account worksheet in Chapter Four as a basis for developing a Frag.

An example of an Account Fragmentary is shown on the following page. Using a Frag helps you understand where you are with the strategic process with each account, as well as providing support specialists—such as account and technical support and clinical affairs managers—with valuable information regarding field issues and challenges and it may clarify ways in which the home office can provide enhanced support to address specific customer and terrain issues.

Chapter Seven Summary

Strategic leadership is based upon a foundation of appropriate and relevant information used wisely. You must collect critical information about all your key accounts:

- Knowledge of yourself, which can be gained by using the Strategic Skills Assessments we've provided

- Knowledge of your competition

- Knowledge of the account terrain

Once you've collected this information, you will be better equipped to know what information can help you succeed with your accounts and what information might be dangerous to reveal, giving your competition a valuable resource and basis for attack.

Information about all levels of your account can also be important. Know who the decision-makers are and where their allegiances lay—and, know the reasons behind those allegiances. The more knowledge you have about motivations and background, the better equipped you will be to make truly strategic, Phase III decisions.

Finally, spend the time needed to plan your account strategy. Use either the long worksheet in Chapter Four or the Account Frag worksheet, which provides a more concise overview of the account and what your strategy is for it. An Account Frag is a good tool for determining quickly where you are with each account, as well as for communicating to account specialists and the home office specific account needs, strengths and weaknesses.

Account Fragmentary

Account Name: _____

Overview of Critical Success Factors and Strategy of this Account

Competition and Competition's Strategy

Objective (SMART):

My Strategy_____

Tactic/Resource	Date	Completed
1.		
2.		
3.		
4.		
5.		

CHAPTER 8

Resources and Self-Reliance

Sun Tzu said: In the operations of war, where there are in the field a thousand swift chariots, as many heavy chariots, and a hundred thousand mail-clad soldiers, with provisions enough to carry them a thousand li, the expenditure at home and at the front, including entertainment of guests, small items such as glue and paint, and sums spent on chariots and armor, will reach the total of a thousand ounces of silver per day. Such is the cost of raising an army of 100,000 men.

We can relate what Sun Tzu says about the cost of running an army to the business management skills required of leaders. In the past, one might be able to make additions to budgets without too much anxiety, but today we have a constant eye on costs and on compliance. Leaders must be much more aware of their overall costs and of how resources are used in the field. Remember, all resource use should directly connect with your strategy. If this isn't the case, then you are probably wasting resources.

When you engage in actual fighting, if victory is long in coming, then men's weapons will grow dull and their ardor will be damped. If you lay siege to a town, you will exhaust your strength.

Again, if the campaign is protracted, the resources of the State will not be equal to the strain.

Now, when your weapons are dulled, your ardor damped, your strength exhausted and your treasure spent, other chieftains will spring up to take advantage of your extremity. Then no man, however wise, will be able to avert the consequences that must ensue.

Thus, though we have heard of stupid haste in war, cleverness has never been seen associated with long delays. There is no instance of a country having benefited from prolonged warfare.

As we saw in Chapter Seven, developing and implementing strategy can appear to be long and drawn-out, but in reality it will compress the sales cycle. As Sun Tzu says, for many reasons we do not want to prolong the process.

An old maxim is that it takes about six or seven calls to advance a sale. A strategist would say that if you accept this premise, you are spending too much time searching for a successful position, which is very inefficient and costly. Also, most customers are looking for focused interactions with sales professionals who understand their issues and local terrain. They do not necessarily want to see you six or seven times when the exact information is covered each time.

The Phase III strategic, consultative sales professional will ensure that he or she knows the customer's critical success factors and strategies before presenting the proposed solution. They will have detailed knowledge of the competition and the terrain, and they will have developed an Account Frag to guide them in following their strategy. The reason sales professionals who are more tactical need six or seven calls to advance the sale is that they have not focused their solutions on what is relevant to the customer. Is it any wonder that our customers are looking for ways to get out of sales calls?

Taking a tactical approach, where you spend time and sales calls looking for an approach that gets the customer's attention, is like laying siege. Remember: "Now, when your weapons are dulled, your ardor damped, your strength exhausted, and your treasure spent, other chieftains will spring up to take advantage of your extremity." This tactical approach makes you less effective and will *decrease* your access to customers.

Imagine instead the impact of starting your presentation by saying something like this:

"For the past several weeks I have had the opportunity to speak with many individuals across your organization. My intention has been to understand the clinical and professional challenges you are facing prior to presenting my solutions. In those interactions with your peers, I have learned that there are several key issues that you all have in common.

"What I would like to do today is to let you know what I have learned, but I would also like to present you with one key attribute of my solution which I feel will address a critical need that I have uncovered."

Tactical approaches that try to gain attention without the appropriate information, without knowing the customer's Critical Success Factors and Strategies, will end up damaging their ability to have significant time and dialogue with the customer in future calls.

The strategist is always learning and always applying what he or she learns to strategic positions. Customers appreciate the time they have with these professionals, and they limit the access of others to make up the difference.

It is only one who is thoroughly acquainted with the evils of war that can thoroughly understand the profitable way of carrying it on.

The skillful soldier does not raise a second levy, neither are his supply-wagons loaded more than twice.

Bring war material with you from home, but forage on the competitor. Thus the army will have food enough for its needs.

Poverty of the State exchequer causes an army to be maintained by contributions from a distance. Contributing to maintain an army at a distance causes the people to be impoverished.

On the other hand, the proximity of an army causes prices to go up; and high prices cause the people's substance to be drained away.

When their substance is drained away, the peasantry will be afflicted by heavy exactions. With this loss of substance and exhaustion of strength, the homes of the people will be stripped bare, and three-tenths of their income will be dissipated; while government expenses for broken chariots, worn-out horses, breast-plates and helmets, bows and arrows, spears and shields, protective mantles, draught-oxen and heavy wagons, will amount to four-tenths of its total revenue. Hence a wise general makes a point of foraging on the competitor. One cartload of the competitor's provisions is equivalent to twenty of one's own, and likewise a single picul of his provender is equivalent to twenty from one's own store.

The strategist builds his or her position on only those resources that he or she can provide personally. If you rely on other resources, you may be in trouble when they are taken away from you. We have all been in situations at the end of the year when the message goes out that expenses must be cut or entertainment curtailed. If you have built your strategy on various types of freebies, you are suddenly in a very tough situation.

As sales and marketing professionals, we might feel that we are not being allowed to compete on a level playing field with competitors who have more of these resources to throw around. As mountain climbers will tell you, you must base your strategy on the premise that you will be alone on the side of the mountain, having to get up or down all by yourself. You climb the mountain as a team, but you must be able, if necessary, to cope unassisted. That is the worst-case scenario, but it could happen.

In sales, base your approach on the resources you control and you will be in a better position. If your competitor has more resources to throw at the opportunity, you can still have success. As the great Samurai, Miyamoto Musashi said in his *Book of Five Rings*, "What does it matter if my competitor has greater resources? If I control the situation, he cannot use them."

Phase III strategists use their knowledge of the customer's situation to provide value that goes beyond the typical Phase II approach. If you have a customer asking for a contribution to a golf outing you cannot afford, the Phase III strategist would let his competitors fund the event, while he took another, more productive approach. The Phase III person might tell the customer:

"I wish I could take out my checkbook and write you a check. That would be a very simple way to support this effort and help cement our relationship. Unfortunately, I don't have that resource available to me. I can, however, give you my commitment that I will constantly look for ways that I can provide value to you by helping you address your objectives — both your clinical objectives and your professional objectives. You can be assured that this will always be my aim with you and your organization, and I hope you see far greater value coming from that type of relationship."

We all have concerns about what we can and cannot do with regard to our customer relationships. The Phase III approach is to take the high road with customers. There can be no concern about quid pro quo when selling strategically. Let others waste their resources. You will feel better about yourself by following the Phase III path, and so will your customers.

Now in order to [overcome] the competitor, our men must be roused to anger; that there may be advantage from defeating the competitor, they must have their rewards.

Therefore in chariot fighting, when ten or more chariots have been taken, those should be rewarded who took the first. Our own flags should be substituted for those of the competitor, and the chariots mingled and used in conjunction with ours. The captured soldiers should be kindly treated and kept. This is called, using the conquered foe to augment one's own strength.

In war, then, let your great object be victory, not lengthy campaigns. Thus it may be known that the leader of armies is the arbiter of the people's fate, the man on whom it depends whether the nation shall be in peace or in peril.

Clearly, incentives drive sales performance. It is important for managers to note, however, Sun Tzu's advice: reward those who get there first. Reward sales excellence—your Phase III strategists. This is doubly important when they are the ones who will be actively recruited by other companies or headhunters. Certainly there are times when teams should be rewarded, such as when objectives are team-centered—but for individuals, it is critical to be sure that they are aware of their value to the company.

Chapter Eight Summary

Strategists ensure that they go into every sales situation fully prepared—to do anything else is to "lay siege" and to court defeat in that customer account. Use the planning tools from earlier in the book to help you be prepared, and go in with an Account Frag to keep you focused on your strategy for each particular account.

In addition, use the resources at your disposal and develop a strategic rationale for using them. Do not feel you have to compete on resources you simply do not have—turn to other advantages you *know* you have and rely on those instead. Assume the worst case— that you are working alone and have only yourself to rely on.

Managers should insist that individuals are recognized for their excellence in a fair way, and that those who are consistent Phase III achievers know their value to the company through appropriate incentives.

CHAPTER 9

Attack by Strategy

Sun Tzu said: in the practical art of war, the best thing of all is to take the competitor's country whole and intact; to shatter and destroy it is not so good. So, too, it is better to recapture an army entire than to destroy it, to capture a regiment, a detachment or a company entire than to destroy them.

Hence to fight and conquer in all your battles is not supreme excellence; supreme excellence consists in breaking the competitor's resistance without fighting.

Thus the highest form of generalship is to balk the competitor's plans; the next best is to prevent the junction of the competitor's forces; the next in order is to attack the competitor's army in the field; and the worst policy of all is to besiege walled cities.

The rule is, not to besiege walled cities if it can possibly be avoided. The preparation of mantlets, movable shelters, and various implements of war, will take up three whole months; and the piling up of mounds over against the walls will take three months more.

The general, unable to control his irritation, will launch his men to the assault like swarming ants, with the result that one-third of his men are slain, while the town still remains untaken. Such are the disastrous effects of a siege.

Therefore the skillful leader subdues the competitor's troops without any fighting; he captures their cities without laying siege to them; he overthrows their kingdom without lengthy operations in the field.

With his forces intact he will dispute the mastery of the Empire, and thus, without losing a man, his triumph will be complete. This is the method of attacking by stratagem.

It is the rule in war, if our forces are ten to the competitor's one, to surround him; if five to one, to attack him; if twice as numerous, to divide our army into two.

If equally matched, we can offer battle; if slightly inferior in numbers, we can avoid the competitor; if quite unequal in every way, we can flee from him.

Hence, though an obstinate fight may be made by a small force, in the end it must be captured by the larger force.

The great and successful strategist is at peak performance when he or she is able to defeat a competitor without having to resort to head-to-head attacks. Since customers are not fond of listening to direct attacks on competitors' products and solutions, there is every reason to try something else. An alternate approach can be based on having overwhelming superiority or on flanking your competitor's position. Remember, strategy is that strength you rely upon to win—and you need to be focused on your strategy rather than relying on attacking your competition.

There are instances where a new product is so far superior to the competition that even the competitor realizes his position is tenuous. An example might be Viagra, whose only competitors at launch were an injectable or a suppository. The mere fact that this new solution was a tablet gave it significant advantages that were very difficult to defend against. When new oral competitors came onto the market, Viagra faced new strategic challenges due to this change in the competitive terrain.

As we have illustrated, the best way to defeat a competitor who already holds the "high ground" with a customer or an account is to flank them. This requires that we identify a weakness in the competitor's position and go for the win there. There are some obstacles to watch out for when taking this approach:

- Since the competitor probably enjoys some support within the account, however, you must be very delicate in how you approach your positioning. If you position your solution as addressing a weakness in your competitor's product, you are less likely to see your customer dig in his heels than if you try a more general attack on the competing product.

- Keep in mind that there are "switching costs" that may affect your ability to supplant a competitor. Switching costs are the tangible and intangible assets that an incumbent builds up with a customer over time. In defining our own positioning, we must include any switching costs that might arise when your product or solution is implemented.

- Taking switching costs into account is important not only because of the customer's financial concerns, but also because we don't want to be vulnerable to the competitor's supporters within the account. If the supporters give our strategy away, we are likely to find ourselves in a head-to-head battle, and offensive strategies are always difficult and resource-intense.

By identifying weaknesses in your competitor's solution and adding your knowledge of how your solution may affect the customer's critical success factors and/or strategy, you will be more likely to get your foot in the door. Thus, a Phase III strategist learns the critical success factors for as many people as possible within the account. This allows you to flank your competitor in ways that he or she would never suspect and, once that happens, you can begin to strengthen your position and protect your product within the account.

Remember, with regard to winning, Sun Tzu says that we might celebrate for a day, but then we must begin again walking around the terrain, learning where we can either improve our position or protect our vulnerable flanks from a competitive move.

Now the general is the bulwark of the State; if the bulwark is complete at all points, the State will be strong; if the bulwark is defective, the State will be weak.

There are three ways in which a ruler can bring misfortune upon his army:

(1) By commanding the army to advance or to retreat, being ignorant of the fact that it cannot obey. This is called hobbling the army.

(2) By attempting to govern an army in the same way as he administers a kingdom, being ignorant of the conditions, which obtain in an army. This causes restlessness in the soldiers' minds.

(3) By employing the officers of his army without discrimination, through ignorance of the military principle of adaptation to circumstances. This shakes the confidence of the soldiers.
But when the army is restless and distrustful, trouble is sure to come from the other feudal princes. This is simply bringing anarchy into the army, and flinging victory away.

Often, the Phase III professionals we work with tell us that the real challenge within their organization is managers who are still ensconced in Phase II. These managers are still immersed in tactics and tend to discount the importance of strategy because they do not understand its value to themselves and their organization or they may feel that "strategy" is something that only comes from the home office.

What advice can we offer managers to move from Phase II to Phase III? Consider the following points—if you are following them, then you are or are moving towards being a Phase III manager:

- Do not press your salespeople simply to be active in making calls—remember, the tactical salesperson searches for messages inefficiently by making too many calls—what Sun Tzu terms "the noise before the defeat." Encourage instead adequate acquisition of information and appropriate planning prior to making strategic sales calls.

- Identify where your sales professionals are on the growth curve—Phase I, II or III—and build plans to advance each individual along the curve to higher strategic understanding.

- With Phase I individuals, remember that they need to first learn the terrain, their own products, and the basics of selling.

- Phase II individuals are moving towards higher levels of trust and understanding with their customers and their peers. They are becoming intuitive in their approach to products and solutions, and they integrate knowledge they've gained about their customers and competitors into the sales dialogue. Managers need to ensure Phase II people don't burn out or lose their edge by setting objectives to help them move away from tactics and towards the focus that real strategy requires.

- Managers should support their Phase III sales professionals with regular feedback and support as they work to develop strategy and tactics based on it. Managers should also challenge their Phase III employees as needed, reviewing how they decided on a particular strategy and how they chose their tactics. If you give your Phase III professionals time to learn their terrain, you'll see a benefit for everyone on the sales team. For example, assigning a Phase III employee to prepare an article on evolving healthcare issues for presentation at a regional or district meeting can encourage similar exploration by advanced Phase II employees.

In summary, successful managers must understand all the concepts of Phase III strategists themselves in order to support their Phase III employees and to develop their Phase I and II employees into more advanced strategic and consultative sales professionals.

Thus we may know that there are five essentials for victory:

(1) He will win who knows when to fight and when not to fight.

(2) He will win who knows how to handle both superior and inferior forces.

(3) He will win whose army is animated by the same spirit throughout all its ranks.

(4) He will win who, prepared himself, waits to take the competitor unprepared.

(5) He will win who has military capacity and is not interfered with by the sovereign.

Hence the saying: If you know the competitor and know yourself, you need not fear the result of a hundred battles. If you know yourself but not the competitor, for every victory gained you will also suffer a defeat.

If you know neither the competitor nor yourself, you will succumb in every battle.

In the lines quoted above, Sun Tzu cites many compelling arguments concerning the need for strategy. A sales organization that understands the strategic process and is involved in developing product strategy will have everybody focused in the same direction. George S. Day talks about this in his book *Market Driven Strategy:* "...your strategy should serve as a central theme that guides and directs the entire team. We are seeking a compass, and not a detailed roadmap."

Being involved in developing these "central themes" and using them to execute competitive positions serves to harness the power of focus. This is how a smaller, strategic organization can overcome a larger, tactical one.

One other way to do this is to use your knowledge of the terrain to tell you when is the right time to mount a competitive move. For example, in a situation where the customer's budgeting process is already completed, and your lab analyzer will require a significant investment of capital, you would prioritize the account accordingly and perhaps not invest time and resources until the next budget cycle. You must learn to translate terrain knowledge into:

• Knowing when to compete

• Knowing how to be prepared

• Knowing how to block interference

• Knowing how to focus

Look again at the fifth item in Sun Tzu's list of the essentials for victory. When you have a strategic organization from top to bottom, it will be very difficult for a competitor to displace you. But this requires inverting the typical organization structure so that those closest to the "action" are in the highest position, with everyone else supporting them. Ensuring that the "sovereign does not interfere" means that if you have the right people in the field serving the customer's needs, you will be successful as long as those farther away don't try to micromanage the customer interaction.

An instructive example is the fiasco that was Jimmy Johnson and Jerry Jones of Dallas Cowboys fame. As the "sovereign," Jerry Jones felt that he should be on the field helping to manage the team even though he had an excellent field strategist in Jimmy Johnson. The frustrations finally became too much for Johnson, and after developing a team that went all the way to winning the Super Bowl, he bailed out.

Chapter Nine Summary

It is best to win without going head-to-head with your competition especially when your force is smaller. If your competitor already holds the high ground, win by flanking them—by identifying a weakness in their position. Once you've identified this, position your solution so it addresses this weakness with your customer rather than mounting a more general attack on the competing product. This flanking activity requires that you be familiar with the Critical Success Factors of your accounts.

Managers should ensure that they are, themselves, Phase III strategists so that they can best support their Phase III sales professionals and have plans in place to develop Phase I and II employees along the continuum to becoming Phase III.

Make sure that your entire sales organization understands the strategic process and is focused in the same strategic direction. Don't try to micromanage interactions with customers; yet know how to use your detailed knowledge of the terrain to determine when it is appropriate to make a competitive move against the competition.

And as a Phase III manager, be certain to set your expectations for your team to understand and execute at a Phase III level. It will take support in the field if you are going to develop your people to this level of performance, and setting the expectation will help to make it clear that you will accept nothing less.

CHAPTER 10

Be Prepared

Sun Tzu said: The good fighters of old first put themselves beyond the possibility of defeat, and then waited for an opportunity of defeating the competitor. To secure ourselves against defeat lies in our own hands, but the opportunity of defeating the competitor is provided by the competitor himself. Thus the good fighter is able to secure himself against defeat, but cannot make certain of defeating the competitor. Hence the saying: One may know how to conquer without being able to do it.

Security against defeat implies defensive tactics; ability to defeat the competitor means taking the offensive. Standing on the defensive indicates insufficient strength; attacking, a superabundance of strength.

The general who is skilled in defense hides in the most secret recesses of the earth; he who is skilled in attack flashes forth from the topmost heights of heaven.

Thus on the one hand we have ability to protect ourselves; on the other, a victory that is complete.

To see victory only when it is within the ken of the common herd is not the acme of excellence. Neither is it the acme of excellence if you fight and conquer and the whole Empire says, "Well done."

To lift an autumn hair is no sign of great strength; to see the sun and moon is no sign of sharp sight; to hear the noise of thunder is no sign of a quick ear.

It is imperative that you know your competition well—Sun Tzu is adamant about this. We ourselves saw the importance of competitive intelligence when we attended the final week of the War College with the U.S. Air Force at Maxwell Air Force Base in Montgomery, Alabama. The War College participants are the best and brightest of the military and private sector and they spend a lot of time analyzing potential competitive attacks so that they can prepare for them.

As a sales professional, you need to ensure that everyone on your sales team is equally as serious when comparing your product solutions with your competitor's. You need to identify clearly the unique strengths and weaknesses of each product or service solution—these strengths, in particular, when they are unique to your product and service capabilities, can become very powerful strategies. You also need to identify the strengths of your competitors and decide how you will address each of them. As General Schwarzkopf said, "...never assume away the capability of your [competitor]." In addition, you need a formal process for evaluating their strengths and weaknesses. You must also practice how to address your own product's weaknesses via blocking tactics and then how you will go on to explain your product's strengths.

At Stovall Grainger, we use WarGaming to identify these strengths and weaknesses. WarGaming provides groups with sample scenarios to investigate, allowing them to discover critical aspects of your and your competitor's organizations and approaches.

What the ancients called a clever fighter is one who not only wins, but excels in winning with ease. Hence his victories bring him neither reputation for wisdom nor credit for courage.
He wins his battles by making no mistakes. Making no mistakes is what establishes the certainty of victory, for it means conquering a competitor that is already defeated.

Hence the skillful fighter puts himself into a position which makes defeat impossible, and does not miss the moment for defeating the competitor.
Thus it is that in war the victorious strategist only seeks battle after the victory has been won, whereas he who is destined to defeat first fights and afterwards looks for victory.

The consummate leader cultivates the moral law, and strictly adheres to method and discipline; thus it is in his power to control success.

Discipline in preparing for a coming battle is a consistent theme throughout Sun Tzu's work. We have talked at length about the need for preparation, including gathering information and analyzing your competitors. Unfortunately, lack of disciplined preparation is all too often the case for sales professionals. Many just do not like to do a lot of pre-planning. We want to be in front of the customer presenting our solutions and closing the sale.

Consider this thought from John Glenn: "The greatest antidote to worry, whether you're getting ready for spaceflight or facing a problem of daily life, is preparation ...the more you try to envision what might happen and what your best response and options are, the more you are able to allay your fears about the future."

For Phase III strategists, there is an additional piece of preparation that is important to include—how you will pull all of this information together to present to your customer. You need to "fight the battle" first in your mind—investing the time you need to capture information, identify your strategy, and plan how to present it.

Purely tactical sales professionals go in to see the customer with very little in the way of a plan, responding to situations as they arise with no "roadmap" for where they are going and how they will get there. If the customer asks them about an issue with their solution, they try to address the weakness and then feel that they should move on to a trial close. Strategists have already prepared for the weakness, so they are prepared both for dealing with the issue and, having gotten over that hurdle, for going back to their own strategy — their winnable position.

In respect of military method, we have, firstly, Measurement; secondly, Estimation of quantity; thirdly, Calculation; fourthly, Balancing of chances; fifthly, Victory.

Measurement owes its existence to Earth; Estimation of quantity to Measurement; Calculation to Estimation of quantity; Balancing of chances to Calculation; and Victory to Balancing of chances. A victorious army opposed to a routed one, is as a pound's weight placed in the scale against single grain.

The onrush of a conquering force is like the bursting of pent-up waters into a chasm a thousand fathoms deep.

There is a "seasonal" pattern to our sales. Initially, our product develops a following, then it attracts competitive attention, leading to a slowing of growth, and finally it begins to lose market share as new competitors enter the field. It's a process similar to a farmer's seasons of planting, nurturing, and harvesting. All products go through these cycles in which we enjoy success for a period and then plateau or decline. The strategic organization realizes this, so they put their efforts behind achieving their objectives earlier in the product lifecycle, and, if not growing market share, at least protecting what they have for a longer period of time.

What can disrupt this pattern is the arrival of someone who decides to play by a new set of rules that include "strategic positioning." When the strategist enters the competition, you see a much more focused effort dedicated to winning and winning quickly through integrating their knowledge of the "terrain." Still, regardless of how strategic an organization is, all products have life cycles.

Chapter Ten Summary

It is critical to know your competition as well as you possibly can, adopting a formal process for evaluating the strengths and weaknesses of competitive products. You must also decide how to address each of these with your customers.

Preparing and practicing for sales calls is also important. This includes planning and rehearsing exactly how you will present all your collected information to your customers.

Products go through "seasonal" cycles that, while never eliminated, are certainly disrupted by the sales strategist, who uses strategy to speed up these cycles.

CHAPTER 11

Using Information

*Sun Tzu said: The control of a
large force is the same principle as
the control of a few men: it is
merely a question of dividing up
their numbers.*

F ighting with a large army under your command is nowise different from
fighting with a small one: it is merely a question of instituting signs and
signals.

What Sun Tzu is talking about here is communication. Fast, effective and
efficient communication is what allows a smaller force to overcome a
larger one. Good communication enables quick shifts in tactics where
necessary, even as everyone on the team stays aligned with the agreed-
upon strategy.

It is critical to communicate marketing and sales strategy effectively and consistently to
the field. Again, we come back to collecting and using relevant information effectively.
Good communication strategy requires that terrain information be collected from all
levels of the organization, not just to ensure that up-to-date terrain knowledge is captured, but also because there must be buy-in from those who will be carrying the message to the customer.

To ensure that your whole host may withstand the brunt of the competitor's attack and remain unshaken — this is effected by maneuvers direct and indirect.

That the impact of your army may be like a grindstone dashed against an egg — this is effected by the science of weak points and strong.

In all fighting, the direct method may be used for joining battle, but indirect methods will be needed in order to secure victory.

Indirect tactics, efficiently applied, are inexhaustible as Heaven and Earth, unending as the flow of rivers and streams; like the sun and moon, they end but to begin anew; like the four seasons, they pass away to return once more.

Often, regardless of how good your resources are, an "indirect" method can work best in a competitive situation.

Case Study: Flanking the Enemy

This is the "indirect" method Sun Tzu is talking about. We worked some years ago with an organization that introduced a new antibiotic used to treat serious infections in hospitalized patients. There were many already-established competitors. Those of you who have sold in this market, know how tough it can be. An analysis of the competitors determined that there was very little that differentiated them. It appeared that most sales were made based on relationships between salespeople and their customers.

Our sales professionals could go directly against the competition, but the competition were tenacious fighters. They already knew the therapeutic area and the customers and you can be sure they had studied our product long before we were even promoting it. What happens when you attack an entrenched competitor? They fight back. Tremendous resources will go into the effort with very little opportunity to establish a foothold.

The one clear differentiator we had was a minor indication in certain pediatric patients. As no one else in our class had that, we decided to use this as our strategy and we were able to flank all competitors with that one differentiating feature. By persuading physicians to start using our antibiotic for the pediatric indication, we helped them develop a comfort level with the product. Of course, sales for that one minor indication would not be sufficient for us to achieve our objectives, so we needed to leverage our initial success into greater use in areas where we were in tighter competition. Based on this strategic entry, however, we were able to build a very successful market position for this product that lasted for years. Because the competition was almost constantly evolving, our own strategies evolved as well, but we established our long-standing success by initially using our point of strength to flank the competitors.

There are not more than five musical notes, yet the combinations of these five give rise to more melodies than can ever be heard.

There are not more than five primary colors (blue, yellow, red, white, and black), yet in combination they produce more hues than can ever be seen. There are not more than five cardinal tastes (sour, acrid, salt, sweet, bitter), yet combinations of them yield more flavors than can ever be tasted.

In battle, there are not more than two methods of attack — the direct and the indirect; yet these two in combination give rise to an endless series of maneuvers. The direct and the indirect lead on to each other in turn. It is like moving in a circle — you never come to an end.

Who can exhaust the possibilities of their combination?

Finding new ways to position their products is one reason Phase III sales professionals suffer burnout less frequently than Phase II reps. Phase III strategists take an approach where they learn something new almost daily that allows them to see new benefits and solutions they can provide to their customers.

When we travel with salespeople, a question we often hear from their customers is, "What's new? What can you tell me about (insert your product name here) that we haven't already talked about 100 times?" The customers of Phase III reps, however, are not hearing the same things over and over again. Recall Sun Tzu's admonition: celebrate a victory for a day, and then the next day start to march around the terrain looking for new ways to improve our position against competitive attacks.

Disney World has signs pointing out "hot spots" for taking scenic photographs. Professional photographers refer to this type of photography as "shooting postcards"— there is nothing arresting in the shots, nothing really special. The professionals and amateurs with a more artistic eye will stay away from these "postcard" spots and look for the perspectives that are rarely noticed by the crowds. That is what sets the experts apart from the casual photographers.

In photography, as in many other arts, anyone can buy the equipment, but it is what you are able to do with it that makes the difference. It is the "soul" that sets certain photographs apart from run-of-the-mill shots. Regardless of how many times a subject has been photographed, those with real skill can find something unique, and that is what creates the "wow."

Phase III sales professionals are able to do exactly this. Drawing on the same resources available to their Phase II peers, they find ways to apply a unique perspective, to use their resources in extraordinary ways. They gain access that allows genuine dialogue and results in success. Phase III strategic professionals have the "soul" that creates real competitive advantage.

The onset of troops is like the rush of a torrent which will even roll stones along in its course. The quality of decision is like the well-timed swoop of a falcon which enables it to strike and destroy its victim.

Therefore the good fighter will be terrible in his onset, and prompt in his decision. Energy may be likened to the bending of a crossbow; decision, to the releasing of a trigger.

Amid the turmoil and tumult of battle, there may be seeming disorder and yet no real disorder at all; amid confusion and chaos, your array may be without head or tail, yet it will be proof against defeat.

Simulated disorder postulates perfect discipline, simulated fear postulates courage; simulated weakness postulates strength.

Hiding order beneath the cloak of disorder is simply a question of subdivision; concealing courage under a show of timidity presupposes a fund of latent energy; masking strength with weakness is to be effected by tactical dispositions.

Thus one who is skillful at keeping the competitor on the move maintains deceitful appearances, according to which the competitor will act. He sacrifices something that the competitor may snatch at it. By holding out baits, he keeps him on the march; then with a body of picked men he lies in wait for him.

The clever combatant looks to the effect of combined energy, and does not require too much from individuals. Hence his ability to pick out the right men and utilize combined energy.

When he utilizes combined energy, his fighting men become as it were like unto rolling logs or stones. For it is the nature of a log or stone to remain motionless on level ground, and to move when on a slope; if four-cornered, to come to a standstill, but if round-shaped, to go rolling down.

Thus the energy developed by good fighting men is as the momentum of a round stone rolled down a mountain thousands of feet in height. So much on the subject of energy.

A well-focused, well-executed strategy is difficult for a competitor to halt. But, as emphasized earlier, the right preparation must go into the effort. Just because we have a well-tested strategy is no guarantee in and of itself that we will achieve our objectives.

As we have seen, it is important to be well prepared. This requires careful planning as we:

- Don't move too quickly—we need to be sure to wait until we know our customer is in a position to commit.

- Don't execute too soon—our competitors may get wind of our position and block our progress while at the same time fortifying their own position.

- Be careful about how and to whom we communicate our strategy—we don't want our message to reach our competition.

It is critical to manage strategic communication. It is especially critical to manage it in accounts that cross more than one local market. How is this situation best managed?

- The individual responsible for the key objective with the opportunity in question should be driving both the strategy and its tactical implementation.

- If you are driving the effort, you may want to tell any tactical, Phase II sales professionals only what they need to do at a local level. If you feel comfortable with the Phase III skills of your team, however, you can involve them in strategy development because they can help you execute it.

- Including Phase III team members at the local and regional levels of a National Account initiative can be very successful. These local and regional team members provide specific terrain information that might be missed at a higher level.

Once you have your entire team focused on your strategy, you see the power that Sun Tzu compares to round stones rolling down a mountain.

Sun Tzu tells us that there is a time to execute strategy and a time to wait; there is a time to communicate your strategy and a time to hold your strategy close. But when you do decide to communicate strategy and/or tactics and to start executing, make sure that you move quickly and with the synergy of your entire team in order to achieve overwhelming force and success. This helps you catch a competitor who is at rest and not prepared.

Case Study: Making Use of Spies

What does Sun Tzu mean when he says that "there may be seeming disorder and yet no real disorder at all"? As an example, consider a bidding situation, or a response to an RFP. Your competitors will probably have their supporters within the account, and these supporters will be passing along everything they learn from you. This might seem like "disorder"—something out of your control. You can, however, create "order" from this situation. A strategist will know who these "spies" are and will include them in his or her tactical plan. The plan will include conversations with the competitive "spies," but the message delivered will be vague and general. It will be the expected position, which the competitor can easily understand. The result will be that the competitor chooses the wrong blocking tactics in their own plan.

This approach can be very effective in large accounts where the competition has several "spies" listening to what you are saying. If each of these "spies" is hearing about some aspect of your solution, and each is being told something a bit different, your competitor will have to block many different possible positions. When you communicate your true strategic advantage — linked in your proposal to influencers' critical success factors and customer strategies — you will flank the competitor, who will never have considered your actual strategy.

Even more powerful is combining this approach with knowledge you have gained in your discussions with your competitor's spies. By listening carefully to their questions, and even drawing them into discussion concerning how they are protecting a particular competitor, you will be able to determine what, if any, strategy your competitor is using. And this is the key to victory. Thus, it is important to listen to what is being said in the account by those who are your "local guides" (which we discuss in detail in upcoming chapters) and those who are competitive "spies." Don't give away your strategy. Don't put your plan into action until the "weather" is favorable. And when you do decide to execute, do so with speed, commitment, and power.

Chapter Eleven Summary

Efficient communication is critical and allows fast tactical shifts when needed, as well as enabling a smaller force to overcome a large one. Be sure to communicate marketing and sales strategy consistently to the field and solicit their input.

When needed and appropriate, use an indirect strategy to flank the enemy. Always be on the lookout for new, unique ways to position your products against your competition.

Be prepared—move at the right time. Effectively manage strategic information. Use "spies" to your advantage by controlling what information they receive. Lay traps and selectively deploy diversionary tactics. Your competition will respond to these deceptive creations while you execute a strategy of which they are unaware.

CHAPTER 12

Know the Enemy

Sun Tzu said: Whoever is first in the field and awaits the coming of the competitor will be fresh for the fight; whoever is second in the field and has to hasten to battle will arrive exhausted.

Therefore the clever combatant imposes his will on the competitor, but does not allow the competitor's will to be imposed on him. By holding out advantages to him, he can cause the competitor to approach of his own accord; or, by inflicting damage, he can make it impossible for the competitor to draw near.

If the competitor is taking his ease, he can harass him; if well supplied with food, he can starve him out; if quietly encamped, he can force him to move. Appear at points which the competitor must hasten to defend; march swiftly to places where you are not expected.

An army may march great distances without distress if it marches through country where the competitor is not. You can be sure of succeeding in your attacks if you only attack places which are undefended. You can ensure the safety of your defense if you only hold positions that cannot be attacked.

Hence that general is skillful in attack whose opponent does not know what to defend; and he is skillful in defense whose opponent does not know what to attack.

O divine art of subtlety and secrecy. Through you we learn to be invisible, through you inaudible; and hence we can hold the competitor's fate in our hands.

You may advance and be absolutely irresistible if you make for the competitor's weak points; you may retire and be safe from pursuit if your movements are more rapid than those of the competitor.

If we wish to fight, the competitor can be forced to an engagement even though he is sheltered behind a high rampart and a deep ditch. All we need do is attack some other place that he will be obliged to relieve.

If we do not wish to fight, we can prevent the competitor from engaging us even though the lines of our encampment are merely traced out on the ground. All we need do is to throw something odd and unaccountable in his way.

By discovering the competitor's dispositions and remaining invisible ourselves, we can keep our forces concentrated, while the competitor's must be divided.

We can form a single united body, while the competitor must split up into fractions. Hence there will be a whole pitted against separate parts of a whole, which means that we shall be many to the competitor's few. And if we are able thus to attack an inferior force with a superior one, our opponents will be in dire straits.

The spot where we intend to fight must not be made known; for then the competitor will have to prepare against a possible attack at several different points; and his forces being thus distributed in many directions, the numbers we shall have to face at any given point will be proportionately few.

For should the competitor strengthen his van, he will weaken his rear; should he strengthen his rear, he will weaken his van; should he strengthen his left, he will weaken his right; should he strengthen his right, he will weaken his left. If he sends reinforcements everywhere, he will everywhere be weak.

Numerical weakness comes from having to prepare against possible attacks; numerical strength, from compelling our adversary to make these preparations against us. Knowing the place and the time of the coming battle, we may concentrate from the greatest distances in order to fight. But if neither time nor place be known, then the left wing will be impotent to succor the right, the right equally impotent to succor the left, the van unable to relieve the rear, or the rear to support the van. How much more so if the furthest portions of the army are anything under a hundred li apart, and even the nearest are separated by several li.

Though according to my estimate the soldiers of Yueh exceed our own in number that shall advantage them nothing in the matter of victory. I say then that victory can be achieved.

Though the competitor is stronger in numbers, we may prevent him from fighting. Scheme so as to discover his plans and the likelihood of their success.
Rouse him, and learn the principle of his activity or inactivity. Force him to reveal himself, so as to find out his vulnerable spots.

Carefully compare the opposing army with your own, so that you may know where strength is superabundant and where it is deficient.

Here, Sun Tzu is telling us to evaluate the competition objectively so we will be ready to control our competitor's tactics and approach. SGI uses competitive War Games to complete this evaluation, to determine how they are likely to attack us or how they will approach the marketplace. We can also determine where they are vulnerable or what areas of pride in their product they will be most inclined to defend. You can do this yourself by gathering the key information we've been talking about regarding self, terrain, and the competition.

With all of this competitive knowledge, we can be ready to control the tactics used by a competitor. How can we do this? For example, suppose we know that our competition is weak with regard to their dosing schedule, while we have a stronger position with regard to our side effects profile. In this case, we might decide to draw the competition into a defensive posture by executing our side effects advantage in dialogue with the customer, but when we leave the customer, we might suggest they ask other salespeople about dosing schedules. This will keep the competition off-balance, and it will give us additional time to properly position and communicate our side effects message.

Knowing our competitor's weaknesses gives us the necessary ammunition to keep them defending against these weaknesses. Since most tactical sales professionals will strongly defend against weaknesses to the detriment of discussing their real strengths, this slows them down significantly. Note that strategists expect to have to answer questions about their solution's weaknesses, and they are prepared to do so. After responding to questions about the weaknesses, however, they move immediately back to their solution's strength. In some situations, they avoid discussion about their weaknesses by promising to come back to the issue later in the discussion. This approach of making sure your strength is clear to the customer, even as a weakness is under discussion, is crucially different from simply responding to the customer's concern. Remember, it's critical to emphasize your strengths.

As an example, let's say that you have a blood glucose meter that takes a bit longer to show the test result, but the accuracy of the result is better. There is a tradeoff here. A competitor may bring up the issue of time-to-result in their discussion with a customer, and then the customer asks you about it in your next meeting. You could address the time-to-result upfront by showing your customer the data indicating that your meter does take slightly longer than the competitor, with the trade-off of greater accuracy. The customer may see the advantage of accuracy as "trumping" the issue of time-to-result.

If you had only addressed the fact that your time-to-result was minimally longer than the competitor's, you might have neutralized that issue but the customer would still see no advantage to using your product rather than the competitor's.

Case Study: Side Effects

We saw this in action while working in the field with a very successful salesperson getting challenged all day about a side effect with his pain medication. He had great access during the day, but he was being confronted with the same question about this side effect in virtually every office.

Now, a strategist would have asked each customer, "What is your experience here?" in order to find out where those attacks were coming from. This particular salesperson did not inquire. Instead, he responded to the concern about the side effect by going to his product information that showed the frequency with which that side effect showed up in clinical trials. After checking that the customer was satisfied with his answer, he asked if the doctor needed more information or patient starters, and we left the call.

Since we were hearing the question about side effects all day long, it didn't take much to see that the salesperson was under attack. At lunch we discussed how he might ask a question or two to test for the physician's experience with the side effect. Our conclusion was that he needed to continue to block the issue, but then he should move to his strategy and put the competitor back on the defensive.

There is also a lesson to be learned here about how a smaller force can control a larger one. A strategic small force knows where they are vulnerable. They are prepared to do what is necessary to avoid battles, or, when engaged, they quickly get around the issue without dwelling on it. They keep their larger competitor off-balance by *making them constantly address their own weaknesses.*

Case Study: The Small Force

Suppose the smaller, strategic company is selling a lab analyzer and has discovered three weaknesses in their competitor's solution: 1) turnaround time, 2) software bugs, and,

3) inflexible contracting terms. The smaller company has also decided that their key advantage (always connected to the customer's clinical and professional needs) is their analyzer's broad test menu, something very different from the competitor's weaknesses.

The strategic salesperson from the smaller company calls on a customer and connects the broad test menu to the customer's needs. The salesperson thereby advances the sales process. But the salesperson also suggests that the customer ask the competitor about their analyzer's turnaround time. In the next call, the salesperson again executes his "breadth of menu" strategy and suggests that the customer address "software bugs" with the competitor. In the next call, the salesperson goes through the same process, but this time suggests the customer ask the competitor about their contracting terms.

During the next couple of days, the competing salesperson is being asked about these three issues by many different customers and learning nothing about your strategy of "breadth of menu." Since she is hearing three different issues, she is unable to decide how to prepare. This is how smaller competitor is controlling a larger one.

In making tactical dispositions, the highest pitch you can attain is to conceal them; conceal your dispositions, and you will be safe from the prying of the subtlest spies, from the machinations of the wisest brains.

How victory may be produced for them out of the competitor's own tactic — that is what the multitude cannot comprehend.

All men can see the tactics whereby I conquer, but what none can see is the strategy out of which victory is evolved.

Do not repeat the tactics which have gained you one victory, but let your methods be regulated by the infinite variety of circumstances. Military tactics are like unto water; for water in its natural course runs away from high places and hastens downwards.

So in war, the way is to avoid what is strong and to strike at what is weak. Water shapes its course according to the nature of the ground over which it flows; the soldier works out his victory in relation to the foe that he is facing.

Therefore, just as water retains no constant shape, so in warfare there are no constant conditions. He who can modify his tactics in relation to his opponent and thereby succeed in winning, may be called a heaven-born captain.

The five elements (water, fire, wood, metal, earth) are not always equally predominant; the four seasons make way for each other in turn. There are short days and long; the moon has its periods of waning and waxing.

It is important to recall the difference between strategy and tactics. Strategy is what we rely upon to win. Tactics are how we communicate the value of our strategy to a specific customer or organization. We need to *stay* focused on our strategy. With our tactics, we need to be *flexible*.

Tactics may thus be different for different customers and influencers in an account, while the final message — the strategic positioning — is the same. Within an individual account, we want all the influencers to be saying the same thing about the solution we are providing.

Case Study: Dealing With Higher Cost

Suppose your product is a cardiovascular device that can help to stabilize a heart attack patient more rapidly than competitive options. This could allow the patient to be moved to an area of less intensive care, or even to be discharged from the hospital more rapidly. However, the cost of your therapy is higher than competitors' costs.

The pharmacy department may resist an increase in their budget to address a "downstream" issue. If your terrain research has uncovered an organizational move to decrease length of stay, emphasizing the positive effect of your device on length of stay might be a strategy that is compelling to everyone involved in influencing the buying decision. A higher-level influencer in the account would refer to this as moving from cost/unit to units/case.

Your tactics—the tools you use to show your solution's effect on length of stay or reduced units per case may be different for the pharmacist, the nursing staff, the cardiac service line manager, and the chief operating officer. But everyone will leave your meeting with the *same* strategy in mind.

Be firm with your strategy, but flexible with your tactics. It is especially important to be firm when you are in the heat of competition but, as great generals will tell you, "no plan outlasts first contact with the enemy." A competitor is not going to be completely predictable, so you may need to change your tactical approach several times during a single day and within a single account. Still, your strategy should always remain the same unless something has changed within the account, with your product, or in the competitive terrain.

Sun Tzu also warns against using the same strategy for every situation that arises with a specific competitor. As we like to say to our marketing department friends, it's the more the merrier as far as potential strategies are concerned. Marketing should always have an array of well-tested strategies among which those closest to particular terrain can choose. Marketing has information that just can't be gathered by the field sales team. Having more strategies to work with gives us many more potential ways to protect our solution's position within the account. Having more potential strategies also makes it very difficult for a competitor to learn what strategy we are using at a specific point in time.

Chapter Twelve Summary

Objectively evaluate your competition to be ready to control their tactics and approach. Competitive wargames can be a useful tool for doing this analysis. Knowing your competition's weaknesses gives you ways to keep them in a defensive position and less focused on their strengths.

Learn to evaluate your strengths versus the competition and use those strengths as strategic positions to gain competitive immunity. Use your strengths as a strategy to keep your competition constantly addressing their own weaknesses and less able to focus on their strengths. Smaller companies can overcome the resources of a larger one by the focused use of strategy, and by identifying and using their competitor's weaknesses.

Stay focused on your strategy but remain flexible in your tactics. Change your tactics as your competition changes but keep your strategy the same *unless* something has changed in your account, with your products, or in the terrain.

CHAPTER 13

Maneuvering

Sun Tzu said: in war, the general receives his commands from the sovereign. Having collected an army and concentrated his forces, he must blend and harmonize the different elements thereof before pitching his camp.

fter that, comes tactical maneuvering, than which there is nothing more difficult. The difficulty of tactical maneuvering consists in turning the devious into the direct, and misfortune into gain.

Regardless of whether or not we are strategists, everyone receives their mission or objectives (their orders) from someone above them, whether it's the Board of Directors, a large stockholder, one's direct sales manager, or some other party at a higher level of authority.

Once we have our objectives, our next move is to get the right people on board to help us achieve them. This means managers need to look for individuals with a Phase III mindset. If your team doesn't have this or you cannot hire them, you need to be able to identify where on the Growth Curve your existing sales professionals are and to move them to higher levels as rapidly as possible. As Sun Tzu says, before we can "pitch our camp," we must be able to identify the strengths and weaknesses of our people, put them into the best positions to succeed, develop our strategies, and prepare to execute those identified strategies. them.

For sales professionals, this means identifying who on your team can most directly help you achieve your objectives. Or, perhaps you will need to identify resources outside your own team—as we saw in Chapter One, there may be others within your customer's organization that you can use to help you reach your objectives.

Thus, to take a long and circuitous route, after enticing the competitor out of the way and though starting after him, to contrive to reach the goal before him, shows knowledge of the artifice of Deviation.

Maneuvering with an army is advantageous; with an undisciplined multitude, most dangerous.

According to Sun Tzu, all competition, including warfare, is won through deception. Remember that in this context, deception means being able to keep the competition guessing about our methods and our strategy, thus preventing them from focusing on their own execution. To achieve this, discipline on the sales team is critical, which is why firm, strategic management is needed.

If the team leader is strategic, then the rest of the team doesn't necessarily need to be— a strategic manager can direct even a Phase I sales team by setting strategy and ensuring the team is focused on the optimal positioning for their product. With a Phase III sales team, a strategic manager can lead the charge by giving them the mission of scouting the terrain, directing certain field activities, handling some key customer interviews, testing account level strategic plans and assisting with resource deployment.

For companies, putting strategic leaders in place will allow them to avoid those "most dangerous" positions.

If you set a fully equipped army in march in order to snatch an advantage, the chances are that you will be too late. On the other hand, to detach a flying column for the purpose involves the sacrifice of its baggage and stores

.

Thus, if you order your men to roll up their buff-coats, and make forced marches without halting day or night, covering double the usual distance at a stretch, doing a hundred li in order to wrest an advantage, the leaders of all your three divisions will fall into the hands of the competitor.

The stronger men will be in front; the jaded ones will fall behind, and on this plan only one-tenth of your army will reach its destination.

If you march fifty li in order to outmaneuver the competitor, you will lose the leader of your first division, and only half your force will reach the goal.

If you march thirty li with the same object, two-thirds of your army will arrive. We may take it then that an army without its baggage-train is lost; without provisions it is lost; without bases of supply it is lost.

We cannot enter into alliances until we are acquainted with the designs of our neighbors. We are not fit to lead an army on the march unless we are familiar with the face of the country — its mountains and forests, its pitfalls and precipices, its marshes and swamps.
We shall be unable to turn natural advantage to account unless we make use of local guides.

Sun Tzu teaches us to be very careful with regard to forming alliances. This admonition has application at all levels of a sales and marketing organization. For example, as we have emphasized previously, we must be careful about how much information we offer to someone at an account before you know something about their personal and professional concerns. Do not give your strategies away to someone who might be a strong supporter of your competition.

Before you form an alliance, you need to become very knowledgeable about the influencers within your account. You need to know their Critical Success Factors and their view of the organization's strategy. This knowledge is a key piece of both knowing the terrain and "making use of local guides"—insiders within your customer's organization.

In war, practice dissimulation, and you will succeed. Whether to concentrate or to divide your troops must be decided by circumstances.

Let your rapidity be that of the wind, your compactness that of the forest. In raiding and plundering be like fire, in immovability like a mountain.

Let your plans be dark and impenetrable as night, and when you move, fall like a thunderbolt.

Be very cautious in developing, communicating, and implementing your strategy. Be conservative in determining to whom to allow this information to be delivered. When you decide to execute your strategy, do it swiftly and with conviction, and be flexible in how you execute your plans tactically. Focused and committed to your strategy, and flexible with your tactics...this is the key to effective and efficient execution.

When you plunder countryside, let the spoil be divided amongst your men; when you capture new territory, cut it up into allotments for the benefit of the soldiery.

When you win a key national or regional account, it is a good idea to share the fruits with all members of the organization. In certain cases, it is important to divide territory after major wins so that the customers can be well served. No salesperson wants to lose a piece of business, so adjustments must be made, but the key here is to ensure that the needs created by new business are not beyond the capabilities of the salesperson handling the account.

Ponder and deliberate before you make a move. He will conquer who has learnt the artifice of deviation. Such is the art of maneuvering.

The Book of Army Management says: On the field of battle, the spoken word does not carry far enough: hence the institution of gongs and drums. Nor can ordinary objects be seen clearly enough: hence the institution of banners and flags.

Gongs and drums, banners and flags, are means whereby the ears and eyes of the host may be focused on one particular point. The host thus forming a single united body, it is impossible either for the brave to advance alone, or for the cowardly to retreat alone. This is the art of handling large masses of men.

In night-fighting, then, make much use of signal-fires and drums, and in fighting by day, of flags and banners, as a means of influencing the ears and eyes of your army.

Even Sun Tzu in his time saw the need for using the most advanced information and communication technology. Today as well, information and communication technology are vital to success in highly competitive markets. While we have the technology, sometimes the way it is used turns its advantage into a hindrance. If email, voicemail and other ways of communicating with management take up too much time, then sales professionals will avoid checking in, communication will suffer, and the direction and execution of strategy will not be as effective. In addition, overly burdensome administrative duties eat into time that sales professionals could otherwise spend with their customers. It is the responsibility of strategic managers to ensure that the communication tools are used appropriately to direct the strategic and tactical efforts of the sales and marketing organizations.

A whole army may be robbed of its spirit; a commander-in-chief may be robbed of his presence of mind.

Now a soldier's spirit is keenest in the morning; by noonday it has begun to flag; and in the evening, his mind is bent only on returning to camp. A clever general, therefore, avoids an army when its spirit is keen, but attacks it when it is sluggish and inclined to return. This is the art of studying moods.

Salespeople have their daily and weekly energy cycles. We particularly remember one salesperson who told us that he was far below the level of energy and motivation he had once had. Now he practiced the "4T's" — "Ten o'clock to Two o'clock, Tuesday through Thursday."

Sun Tzu's message here can also be applied to the product lifecycle. When a product is new, there will be great energy among the sales force. When the newness wears off, there is a danger that flagging energy will begin opening opportunities for competitors, so both sales professionals and their managers need to find ways of re-energizing their sense of mission.

Disciplined and calm, to await the appearance of disorder and hubbub amongst the competitor this is the art of retaining self-possession.

To be near the goal while the competitor is still far from it, to wait at ease while the competitor is toiling and struggling, to be well-fed while the competition is famished: this is the art of husbanding one's strength.

If we are faced with limited resources, we must use them wisely. Direct your resources only toward achieving objectives where you have learned your customers' critical success factors and strategies. Avoid being in too much of a rush—rushing is easily spotted by competitors and customers and they will sense when we are pushing too hard for the close, whether we are or not.

Trying to move too fast will lessen your customers' willingness to have dialogue with you. If you have a thoroughly considered plan and execute it well, however, you can reach your objectives before the competition. This puts the pressure on them while you retain access to your customers.

To refrain from intercepting a competitor whose banners are in perfect order, to refrain from attacking an army drawn up in calm and confident array: this is the art of studying circumstances.

It is a military axiom not to advance uphill against the competitor, nor to oppose him when he comes downhill. Do not pursue a competitor who simulates flight; do not attack soldiers whose temper is keen. Do not swallow bait offered by the competitor. Do not interfere with an army that is returning home.

When you surround an army, leave an outlet free. Do not press a desperate foe too hard. Such is the art of warfare.

Remember the wisdom of avoiding direct attack on a competitor? There are several reasons this is not a good tactical approach. We find that many customers tell us that sales professionals who criticize a competitive product that the customer is currently using are seen as attacking the *decision* the customer made. This is an especially undesirable outcome with very analytical clinicians.

Instead of asking your customer to replace completely what they are currently using or doing, ask them to evaluate your proposed solution in a specific area—one where their selection might have a weakness addressing a clinical and/or business challenge. By doing this, you are not asking them to abandon their current choice except in this one area. Once your customer sees your solution offers significant advantages in the area you've cited, they will be much more open to seeing how your solution might assist them in other areas. This is the essence of a "flanking" strategy: positioning your product's strength against a competitor's weakness.

Chapter Thirteen Summary

Identify appropriate resources and team members to support your objective—management should be prepared to train sales professionals who are not yet at Phase III and set the expectation that this is the way business opportunities will be approached. If your team leader is strategic, then the rest of the team does not need to be—strategic leaders can ensure the strategy is communicated and the team remains focused on it. Putting Phase III team leaders in place will avoid Sun Tzu's "most dangerous positions." However, since the team leader is unable to have the day-to-day direct customer contact that a field representative can, a much more effective organization would include strategists at all levels. At a minimum, the team leaders must be strategic.

Forming alliances requires caution and in depth knowledge of the terrain. At the same time, be cautious about communicating your strategy.

A direct attack on a product currently being used by one of your target customers is an insult to the customer. Strategists always avoid these direct attacks.

CHAPTER 14

Variation in Tactics

Sun Tzu said: in war, the general receives his commands from the sovereign, collects his army and concentrates his forces.

F ield sales managers receive their objectives from their own managers, but executing strategy is most successful when the responsibility for directing efforts in the field is left to them. This again underscores the need for all management to be strategic, for strategists understand this and can manage their field sales professionals according to where they are on the Phase I through III Growth Curve.

When in difficult country, do not encamp. In country where high roads intersect, join hands with your allies.

Do not linger in dangerously isolated positions. In hemmed-in situations, you must resort to stratagem. In desperate position, you must fight.

There are roads which must not be followed, armies which must be not attacked, towns which must not be besieged, positions which must not be contested, and commands of the sovereign which must not be obeyed.

Field sales management is complex. Managers are responsible for facilitating, developing, communicating, testing, and implementing strategy in an environment in which constant change and active competition are givens. This means that adjustments to the tactical side of the plan must be made rapidly and accurately. Thus, the field leader must simultaneously keep the team focused with the strategy, while also letting them know that they will be required to make tactical adjustments as and when necessary.

A good Phase III manager realizes that if every decision must pass through him or her, the team may be frustrated in their efforts and flanked by their competitors. The Allied D-Day invasion of World War II offers a good analogy—while the invasion strategy was clear, poor weather, bad seas, missed jumps, and many changes in terrain situations compelled the troops to adjust on the fly. Fortunately, those executing the invasion knew what their objectives were and they made the required adjustments in order to achieve their objectives even in the face of intense attacks by entrenched enemy troops.

Field sales must know to stay focused on their strategy even when it seems as if everything is falling apart. They do this by focusing on their objectives and adjusting their tactics to the current terrain.

The general who thoroughly understands the advantages that accompany variation of tactics knows how to handle his troops.

The general who does not understand these may be well acquainted with the configuration of the country, yet he will not be able to turn his knowledge to practical account.

So, the student of war who is unversed in the art of war of varying his plans, even though he is acquainted with the Five Advantages, will fail to make the best use of his men.

There are various levels of strategic understanding. What Sun Tzu is saying here is that you may be knowledgeable about objectives, strategy, tactics, and resource deployment, but such "academic" understanding does not necessarily translate into effective action. We describe this type of individual as "skilled in the operational arts"— someone able to talk the talk, but unable consistently to walk the talk. The latter requires knowing how to redeploy effectively when change forces us to make adjustments to our tactical approach. Being too married to a tactical plan can lead to failure.

Strategists are constantly measuring their understanding of self, other, and terrain to ensure that they are moving toward achieving their objectives. For the most part, this leads to adjusting tactics only and not strategy.

Hence in the wise leader's plans, considerations of advantage and of disadvantage will be blended together. If our expectation of advantage be tempered in this way, we may succeed in accomplishing the essential part of our schemes.

If, on the other hand, in the midst of difficulties we are always ready to seize an advantage, we may extricate ourselves from misfortune.

Reduce the hostile chiefs by inflicting damage on them, and make trouble for them, and keep them constantly engaged; hold out specious allurements, and make them rush to any given point.

The art of war teaches us to rely not on the likelihood of the competitor's not coming, but on our own readiness to receive him; not on the chance of his not attacking, but rather on the fact that we have made our position unassailable.

As General Norman Schwarzkopf said, "never assume away the capability of your [competitor]." There is a tendency for us to believe so strongly in our solution's advantages that we just cannot imagine a competitor having an effective position against us. Sun Tzu cautions us against relying on any strength or capability or assumption about the competition. Instead, he advises, rely on *our* preparation, on the information we've gathered ourselves, on our access to our own customers, on building *our* competitive immunity. By strengthening our position—our strategy and tactics—we can be ready to adapt when needed to meet and resist our competition's attacks.

There are five dangerous faults which may affect a general:

(1) Recklessness, which leads to destruction;

(2) Cowardice, which leads to capture;

(3) A hasty temper, which can be provoked by insults;

(4) A delicacy of honor which is sensitive to shame;

(5) Over-solicitude for his men, which exposes him to worry and trouble.

These are the five besetting sins of a general, ruinous to the conduct of war. When an army is overthrown and its leader slain, the cause will surely be found among these five dangerous faults. Let them be a subject of meditation.

First—a leader or manager who shortchanges the three prerequisites to strategy — knowledge of self, other, and terrain — will destroy the chance for full success in an account. It may not happen today, but sooner or later a competitor will flank him.

Second—managers must be willing to challenge assigned tactics that do not align with the account strategy. If this does not happen, if the manager pursues tactics that do not support the strategy, then the account opportunity is built on weakness, not strength, and will be vulnerable to competitors.

Managers must be on the lookout for projects or tactics mandated by the organization that are off-strategy. She must be able to articulate her concerns clearly in order to convey the potential harmful consequences of such tactics—and if she does this successfully they will, in most cases, be dropped.

Third—Sun Tzu tells us that if our competitor is quick to lose his temper, then provoke him. This idea applies to us as well as our competitor. Specifically, if a manager cannot control his temper, he will be less effective. The team will avoid revealing bad news because they don't want to face their manager's wrath. Shutting down communication in this way means that an obstacle remains unaddressed that might be overcome by adjusting tactics.

Fourth—Phase III salespeople do not take failure as a personal attack. There are situations in which we are not going to win regardless of how strategically we approach the challenge. If we feel that a sales loss is a customer's personal attack on us, we may shy away from highly competitive but very lucrative sales opportunities.

Fifth—managers must also be very careful about becoming so emotionally involved with their sales team that they cannot separate the performance from the individual. If a salesperson is not achieving his or her objectives, the manager must be willing to address that shortcoming without feeling that he is attacking the person.

Chapter Fourteen Summary

Sun Tzu again emphasizes the need for and advantages of strategic leadership—in sales, strategic managers are better able to direct field sales professionals or bring them along the growth curve when they.

One responsibility of management is to communicate strategy clearly so that the team knows its objectives. This allows them to adjust tactics when there are changes in the situation or terrain.

Strategic understanding includes not just a high level understanding but also the knowledge of how to translate this into effective actions.

Sun Tzu suggests we avoid reliance on any of our competition's traits of capabilities and, instead, rely on our own. It is our own preparation, resources, information and relationship with the customer that will win the account in the long term.

Managers need to avoid five dangerous faults by doing the following:

• Taking time to gather knowledge you need

• Being willing to challenge assigned tactics not aligned with strategy

• Controlling our tempers

• Not taking failure as a personal attack

• Staying objective so you are able to separate performance from the individual.

CHAPTER 15

Observing Signs of the Competitor

Sun Tzu said: We come now to the question of encamping the army and observing signs of the competitor.

P ass quickly over mountains, and keep in the neighborhood of valleys. Camp in high places, facing the sun. Do not climb heights in order to fight. So much for mountain warfare.

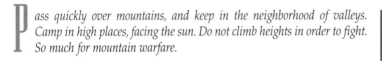

After crossing a river, you should get far away from it. When an invading force crosses a river in its onward march, do not advance to meet it in mid-stream. It will be best to let half the army get across, and then deliver your attack.

If you are anxious to fight, you should not go to meet the invader near a river which he has to cross. Moor your craft higher up than the competitor and facing the sun. Do not move upstream to meet the competitor. So much for river warfare.

In crossing salt marshes, your sole concern should be to get over them quickly, without any delay. If forced to fight in a salt marsh, you should have water and grass near you, and get your back to a clump of trees. So much for operations in salt marshes.

In dry, level country, take up an easily accessible position with rising ground to your right and on your rear, so that the danger may be in front, and safety lie behind. So much for campaigning in flat country.

These are the four useful branches of military knowledge which enabled the Yellow Emperor to vanquish four several sovereigns.

All armies prefer high ground to low and sunny places to dark. If you are careful of your men and camp on hard ground, the army will be free from disease of every kind, and this will spell victory.

When you come to a hill or a bank, occupy the sunny side, with the slope on your right rear. Thus you will at once act for the benefit of your soldiers and utilize the natural advantages of the ground.

When, in consequence of heavy rains up-country, a river which you wish to ford is swollen and flecked with foam, you must wait until it subsides.

Country in which there are precipitous cliffs with torrents running between, deep natural hollows, confined places, tangled thickets, quagmires and crevasses, should be left with all possible speed and not approached.

While we keep away from such places, we should get the competitor to approach them; while we face them, we should let the competitor have them on his rear. If in the neighborhood of your camp there should be any hilly country, ponds surrounded by aquatic grass, hollow basins filled with reeds, or woods with thick undergrowth, they must be carefully routed out and searched; for these are places where men in ambush or insidious spies are likely to be lurking.

When the competitor is close at hand and remains quiet, he is relying on the natural strength of his position. When he keeps aloof and tries to provoke a battle, he is anxious for the other side to advance. If his place of encampment is easy of access, he is tendering a bait.

Movement amongst the trees of a forest shows that the competitor is advancing. The appearance of a number of screens in the midst of thick grass means that the competitor wants to make us suspicious. The rising of birds in their flight is the sign of an ambuscade. Startled beasts indicate that a sudden attack is coming.

When there is dust rising in a high column, it is the sign of chariots advancing; when the dust is low, but spread over a wide area, it betokens the approach of infantry. When it branches out in different directions, it shows that parties have been sent to collect firewood.

A few clouds of dust moving to and fro signify that the army is encamping.

Humble words and increased preparations are signs that the competitor is about to advance.

Violent language and driving forward as if to the attack are signs that he will retreat.

When the light chariots come out first and take up a position on the wings, it is a sign that the competitor is forming for battle.

Peace proposals unaccompanied by a sworn covenant indicate a plot.

When there is much running about and the soldiers fall into rank, it means that the critical moment has come.

When some are seen advancing and some retreating, it is a lure.

When the soldiers stand leaning on their spears, they are faint from want of food.

If those who are sent to draw water begin by drinking themselves, the army is suffering from thirst.

If the competitor sees an advantage to be gained and makes no effort to secure it, the soldiers are exhausted.

If birds gather on any spot, it is unoccupied.

Clamor by night betokens nervousness.

If there is disturbance in the camp, the general's authority is weak. If the banners and flags are shifted about, sedition is afoot. If the officers are angry, it means that the men are weary.

When an army feeds its horses with grain and kills its cattle for food, and when the men do not hang their cooking-pots over the camp-fires, showing that they will not return to their tents, you may know that they are determined to fight to the death.

The sight of men whispering together in small knots or speaking in subdued tones points to disaffection amongst the rank and file.

Sun Tzu speaks often about the need to fully *know* the terrain. This is a common mistake sales professionals make—they feel they can rest once they have won the business. Instead, Sun Tzu admonishes us to begin walking around the territory immediately looking for areas where we might now be attacked and for opportunities to bolster our defenses.

This means that strategists who have won business immediately begin to develop new defensive positions for that business. By continuing to gather relevant information about our customer's issues and learn the Critical Success Factors of influencers around the account, we will be able to continue to connect our solution to high-level needs even as those needs evolve, reinforcing our current position and protecting ourselves from competitors.

We must also pay close attention to competitive tactics. Listen to what competitors are saying in the account by involving your "local guides." This will help you decide how to reinforce your key positions and prepare yourself for attacks. For example, you might learn that a competitor is devoting considerable effort to a specific product or is executing a particular strategy (delivering a particular positioning message) for a product at the expense of their other solutions. This would be a helpful clue that the competing salespeople are being pushed to succeed with this particular product above others, something that you would want to defend against and helping you see where to concentrate your efforts.

As the great samurai Miyamoto Musashi said, when it comes to your competitors, you must "pay attention to trifles." Even small changes and bits of information about the competition and your customers can help you position yourself better.

Too frequent rewards signify that the competitor is at the end of his resources; too many punishments betray a condition of dire distress.

Offering significant changes in bonus structures or incentives will send a message to the competition and your own field sales professionals that something big is happening and that the organization might be in trouble. For example, if the directive is given to increase call activity without a strategic context, Phase III professionals will interpret it as a signal that either product sales are not acceptable, or that something else is afoot in the home office.

Sun Tzu tells us to notice when such situations arise with our competitors because they are signs of weakness. When you are faced with dealing with this situation yourself, stay focused on your strategy and calm in your approach. Your customers can sense added pressure and tend to avoid having to deal with representatives who exhibit signs of stress. The better you manage tactical pressures, the more easily you will maintain access to your customers. Just be prepared to competitively block and trap where necessary.

To begin by bluster, but afterwards to take fright at the competitor's numbers, shows a supreme lack of intelligence

When envoys are sent with compliments in their mouths, it is a sign that the competitor wishes for a truce.

If the competitor's troops march up angrily and remain facing ours for a long time without either joining battle or taking themselves off again, the situation is one that demands great vigilance and circumspection.

If our troops are no more in number than the competitor, that is amply sufficient; it only means that no direct attack can be made. What we can do is simply to concentrate all our available strength, keep a close watch on the competitor, and obtain reinforcements.

He who exercises no forethought but makes light of his opponents is sure to be captured by them.

If you underestimate your competitors, they are likely to flank you. Competitors have products that enjoy winning positions too—if you assume that they have no strategic advantages over you, you will very likely be defeated. That's why strategists always prepare for the "nightmare scenario." What is the worst case scenario for you versus a competitor? One way we like to look at this question is to consider how one of our strongest team members would attack us if she went over to the competition.

If soldiers are punished before they have grown attached to you, they will not prove submissive; and, unless submissive, then will be practically useless. If, when the soldiers have become attached to you, punishments are not enforced, they will still be useless.
Therefore soldiers must be treated in the first instance with humanity, but kept under control by means of iron discipline. This is a certain road to victory.

If in training soldiers commands are habitually enforced, the army will be well disciplined; if not, its discipline will be bad.

If a general shows confidence in his men but always insists on his orders being obeyed, the gain will be mutual.

Sales management has its own difficult challenges with regard both to managing the business and leading the sales team. SGI's Active Leadership I and II workshop were developed to help managers and leaders to improve their "people leadership" knowledge and skills. (See more on this at our website: www.sgbci.com.) Sun Tzu indicates that there must be a period of indoctrination during which the salesperson is able to connect with his or her sales management and the rest of the team. The salesperson must understand that there is a "growth period" expected, and that a supportive mentor will be around to help throughout this transitional period.

As sales professionals grow in experience and strategic knowledge, they know that there are expectations for them to achieve their objectives, complete reports, update and communicate customer records, and capture strategic and tactical information for others to peruse. Discipline in these areas is fundamental to a successful team. Consistency in the way you work with your team and in how you communicate expectations will help you overcome shortcomings before they seriously detract from your team's odds of success. You must clearly set objective standards and expectations around integrity and loyalty from the beginning and ensure that everyone is onboard. And when your team is successful, don't let their success make them complacent.

Good leaders are able to respond to difficult sales situations without being dogmatic, while also being strict enough to hold team members accountable for achieving agreed objectives and developing up-to-date strategic account plans.

Chapter Fifteen Summary

Never stop gathering terrain information, especially after a win. This is the time to develop new defensive positions. Remember the Phase III, strategic consultative sales professional is always either executing strategy or learning the terrain.

Take care in adopting extreme tactics such as significant changes in incentives—this can suggest to your competitors and reps that the organization or project is in trouble.

Consider all the ways your competition can attack you, and prepare for the worst in order to have the most complete and effective defense

CHAPTER 16

Terrain

Sun Tzu said: We may distinguish six kinds of terrain, to wit:

(1) Accessible ground;

(2) Entangling ground;

(3) Temporizing ground;

(4) Narrow passes;

(5) Precipitous heights;

(6) Positions at a great distance from the competitor.

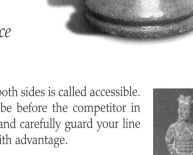

round which can be freely traversed by both sides is called accessible. With regard to ground of this nature, be before the competitor in occupying the raised and sunny spots, and carefully guard your line of supplies. Then you will be able to fight with advantage.

Sun Tzu's definition of "accessible" ground is analogous to a dual contract situation at a healthcare organization. The customer might feel for various reasons that they will not allow one company to enjoy exclusivity, so they award a dual contract. In this situation you should accept the reality and focus on gaining a disproportionate share — 50 percent or more. Concentrate on finding the product positions that are easiest for you to support, and try to determine where you will enjoy the greatest success — the "sunny" spots. If you can do this early in the contract period, it gives you a stronger position from which to grow your share.

It will also be important for you to gain access to higher-level influencers in the account so that you can uncover their critical success factors. With that new information, and with this added access, you will find new ways to connect your solutions to bigger issues within the account. You can then show your customer how your solution is helping to address not just the obvious issues, but also higher-level goals of individuals at the account.

Ground which can be abandoned but is hard to re-occupy is called entangling. From a position of this sort, if the competitor is unprepared, you may sally forth and defeat him. But if the competitor is prepared for your coming, and you fail to defeat him, then, return being impossible, disaster will ensue.

Many sales professionals who find they are blocked in an account by buying resistance at the traditional user level decide to go around the user. They worry, however, about whether this approach will work and they are right to worry. It is very easy for a person at the user level — e.g., a pharmacy director, radiology department head, or lab director — to sabotage your product's success if they feel that you have gone around them. If a competitor is entrenched in the department, and they learn that you are trying to go around the department head, they are likely to make a point of telling the person you have bypassed to try to ensure that you get called on the carpet.

Still, if the user is not allowing you to present your solution, you may have no other choice than to go around them and then deal with the consequences later. Just be sure that you unseat the competitor effectively so that the competitor cannot try to thwart your product's success. If the competitor does remain in the account, they will use your tactical maneuvering against you, and you may find yourself alienating the user-level customer.

On the other hand, if you are able to flank a user-level person who is supporting the competitor and completely unseat the competition, you may be able to come back to the user and rebuild the relationship. In this situation you will have to use strong relationship skills to show the user that you never intended to negate their interests.

Another way to deal with "entangling ground" is to position yourself as a solution *only where* the established competitor is truly weak. If you can get the user-level influencer to see how this is a logical move, you can develop a foothold that you can expand later, once the user sees that you have delivered on your promise in of it the initial area of strength. And if you are able to connect your solution to a higher level critical success factor or an organizational strategy, you have an even greater opportunity to win.

When the position is such that neither side will gain by making the first move, it is called temporizing ground. In a position of this sort, even though the competitor should offer us an attrac-

tive bait, it will be advisable not to stir forth, but rather to retreat, thus enticing the competitor in his turn; then, when part of his army has come out, we may deliver our attack with advantage.

With regard to narrow passes, if you can occupy them first, let them be strongly garrisoned and await the advent of the competitor. Should the army forestall you in occupying a pass, do not go after him if the pass is fully garrisoned, but only if it is weakly garrisoned.

With regard to precipitous heights, if you are beforehand with your adversary, you should occupy the raised and sunny spots, and there wait for him to come up. If the competitor has occupied them before you, do not follow him, but retreat and try to entice him away.
If you are situated at a great distance from the competitor, and the strength of the two armies is equal, it is not easy to provoke a battle, and fighting will be to your disadvantage.

First-mover positioning is ideal. As first-mover, you are able to establish your product as the innovator in its category. That is why we say that innovation is a strategy that cannot be defended against. First-mover advantage helps you occupy the "high ground" within an account.

Conversely, heed Sun Tzu's admonition to avoid making a hasty assault if it is the competitor who has gained the high ground. Instead, it is best to use a flanking strategy to displace a competitor who has established the high ground advantage.

In literal terms, when a competitor has the high ground, he is able to see the competition coming and can prepare his defenses. In figurative terms, a competitor who has occupied the "high ground" of innovation in a category is hard to displace because the customer doesn't want to keep making changes in her protocols. The customer may, for example, let the holder of the "high ground"—the first mover—know what you are saying in your attempts to displace his solution. This gives your competition the advantage since he can then defend his product or solution from a position of strength.

These six are the principles connected with Earth. The general who has attained a responsible post must be careful to study them.

Now an army is exposed to six several calamities, not arising from natural causes, but from faults for which the general is responsible. These are: 1) Flight; (2) insubordination; (3) collapse; (4) ruin; (5) disorganization; (6) rout.

Other conditions being equal, if one force is hurled against another ten times its size, the result will be the flight of the former.

When the common soldiers are too strong and their officers too weak, the result is insubordination.

When the officers are too strong and the common soldiers too weak, the result is collapse.

When the higher officers are angry and insubordinate, and on meeting the competitor give battle on their own account from a feeling of resentment, before the commander-in-chief can tell whether or not he is in a position to fight, the result is ruin.

When the general is weak and without authority, when his orders are not clear and distinct, when there are no fixed duties assigned to officers and men, and the ranks are formed in a slovenly haphazard manner, the result is utter disorganization.

When a general, unable to estimate the competitor's strength, allows an inferior force to engage a larger one, or hurls a weak detachment against a powerful one, and neglects to place picked soldiers in the front rank, the result must be rout.

These are six ways of courting defeat, which must be carefully noted by the general who has attained a responsible post.

Managers are responsible for the actions of their sales teams. They must position their teams so that they have the greatest opportunity to win, and avoid putting them into situations that are futile. A manager who has the respect of the team can count on achievements on a grand scale.

Sun Tzu is very clear that a general must set clear objectives, train the "troops" so that they understand what they are expected to do tactically, and then measure the results. If a manager does not follow through on his or her expectations, whether or not the agreed-upon objectives have been achieved, the team will lack the discipline necessary for success.

So managers have a difficult task. They must know where each member of the team is on the Growth Curve, develop the team so that they move along the curve as quickly as possible, and set high but reasonable expectations. We recommend placing Phase III team members in positions of team leadership (either formally or informally) because you can expect the rest of the team to be supportive, and the Phase III people will feel empowered.

The natural formation of the country is the soldier's best ally; but a power of estimating the adversary, of controlling the forces of victory, and of shrewdly calculating difficulties, dangers and distances, constitutes the test of a great general.

He who knows these things, and in fighting puts his knowledge into practice, will win his battles. He who knows them not, nor practices them, will surely be defeated.

Knowledge is the key to success in strategy development. If a sales team falls short in gathering and using information about self, other, and terrain, they risk losing to a Phase III competitor. Phase III strategic sales professionals succeed where others fail because they gather thorough knowledge and consistently put this knowledge to work (as opposed to treating information gathering as simply an academic exercise).

A clear concern here is whether or not your "generals" are truly strategic. Organizations cannot long afford to have tactical rather than strategic sales managers. Several studies have been done to measure the effects of ineffective management on a company's bottom line, including some by the Challey Group and McKinsey ("Making More of Pharma's Sales Force," The McKinsey Quarterly #3, 2002). In this study, it was shown that 87 percent of training is wasted when not supported by field management. This raises a key question: Can all of your managers support the strategic process?

If fighting is sure to result in victory, then you must fight, even though the ruler forbid it; if fighting will not result in victory, then you must not fight even at the ruler's bidding.

A Phase III sales professional must be allowed to make decisions in "the heat of battle." As we've seen, one of the reasons the D-Day invasion was so successful against an entrenched, battle-hardened German force was that the Allied troops were able to make decisions on their own while the battle was underway. They knew what their objectives were in advance, so although they sometimes landed miles away from where their commanders had planned, they were able to adjust and move effectively based on what they saw happening in the terrain and at that moment. Meanwhile, the German troops had to wait for any changes in their tactics to be approved by someone far behind the lines.

For those of us selling in the field, it is not uncommon to hear something that indicates the time has come to execute our strategy immediately with a particular customer. We must be able to make decisions and respond quickly to opportunities, therefore, without having to pass everything through what one writer has called"the corporate colon." We must also, however, earn the right to make such decisions at the field level by showing we are responsible in our actions.

A more challenging situation is when we decide *not* to exploit an opportunity with a customer despite knowing that corporate expects us to do so. For example, we frequently hear sales professionals protest about the need to"load" product in at the end of a quarter in order to meet their sales objectives. Though some customers may welcome the chance to purchase because they are being offered better pricing or contracting terms, other customers may resent what they perceive as undue pressure to place an order. In situations in which a Phase III sales professional feels that"pushing" a customer to make this kind of a purchase will damage their relationship, he or she should consider alternatives to the corporate mandate. Sustaining a healthy long-term relationship with the customer will provide more value over time than making sales in the short term. For example, if the current marketing brocure is focused on lower cost per unit and the customer is more concerned about reducing length of stay, then executing the cost per unit strategy may be uninteresting to your influencer.

In Michael Porter and Elisabeth Teisberg's book *Redefining Healthcare,* they mention that more progressive sales organizations must be willing to walk away from opportunities when what the customer is already doing is sufficient to the task. Change for change's sake is not enough. It is most important to understand how our customer measures success, be it outcomes, efficiency, or impact on care at the condition level. Knowing this allows Phase III professionals to better position their solutions where they are most appropriate. Clearly, customer specific strategies will always trump general strategies.

As an example, we often hear physicians say that it would be best if sales professionals had a broader understanding of their individual practice needs before they ever mentioned their products. One specific comment from a physician at a prestigious organization was,"I don't want to see some brochure with general information about a product. I just want to see how a product can better meet the needs of my patients based on what I am currently using."

The general who advances without coveting fame and retreats without fearing disgrace, whose only thought is to protect his country to do good service for his sovereign, is the jewel of the kingdom.

Phase III strategic sales professionals keep the needs of their customers' front and center while simultaneously working diligently to achieve their organizations' objectives. They do not get involved in power plays, either in the customer's organization or in their own, and because of this they gain a reputation for integrity. In turn, customers grow to appreciate this kind of service and will look for ways to help the Phase III sales professional succeed, opening up new opportunities to the salesperson and recommending them to others who might use their services

Kenichi Ohmae said it very clearly in his book, *The Mind of the Strategist*: "…theories and concepts are subject to obsolescence but brains and thought processes are not. In a competitive marketplace, the mind of the strategist is an asset that always appreciates in value."

Regard your soldiers as your children, and they will follow you into the deepest valleys; look upon them as your own beloved sons, and they will stand by you even unto death
.
If, however, you are indulgent, but unable to make your authority felt; kind-hearted, but unable to enforce your commands; and incapable, moreover, of quelling disorder: then your soldiers must be likened to spoilt children; they are useless for any practical purpose.

The strategic, Phase III approach is not an easy one. Unless you are feeling some discomfort using Phase II skills, you may not want to accept the challenge of moving to Phase III. Still, the complexities of the healthcare marketplace dictate that the Phase III skill set will be necessary for success. What does this mean for the sales manager, who must work to develop and implement the strategic process in the sales team?

We see all levels of commitment when we provide training for sales and marketing professionals. On one end of the spectrum, we see individuals who pick up on the personal and professional value they can gain from being strategic. These people are eager to get back in the field and begin to exercise these new skills.

At the other end of the spectrum are individuals who are none too eager to implement anything new. When the strategic approach requires them to move out of their comfort zone, they come up with endless excuses for delaying application of the concepts they've learned. It is imperative that companies hire and promote Phase III managers who can facilitate and motivate reluctant team members to begin practicing Phase III skills.

To lead their teams and manage their assigned business effectively, managers must be able to earn the respect of their people, set expectations that challenge the team, and make those expectations stick when assessing performance. If resistant Phase II people feel that they can get around their manager's expectations, they will do everything they can to defer meeting Phase III criteria. This behavior is professionally damaging for the individual and debilitating for the team.

If we know that our own men are in a condition to attack, but are unaware that the competitor is not open to attack, we have gone only halfway towards victory.

If we know that the competitor is open to attack, but are unaware that our own men are not in a condition to attack, we have gone only halfway towards victory.

If we know that the competitor is open to attack, and also know that our men are in a condition to attack, but are unaware that the nature of the ground makes fighting impracticable, we have still gone only halfway towards victory.

Hence the experienced soldier, once in motion, is never bewildered; once he has broken camp, he is never at a loss.

Hence the saying: If you know the competitor and know yourself, your victory will not stand in doubt; if you know Heaven and know Earth, you may make your victory complete.

Managers must also determine where each member of the sales team is on the Growth Curve, develop training plans to move team members along the curve, continue to challenge and develop each member's individual skills and talents, and set expectations that challenge each person to execute.

When managers have people at all levels of development within the Growth Curve, they must work with each individual at his or her current level, never setting expectations that are beyond the next level of growth. For Phase I people, this means the manager generally sets the strategic direction and assigns tactical goals. The manager keeps the salesperson out of situations (such as dealing with difficult customers) in which they might suffer severe consequences from their tactical naivety.

For Phase II people, the manager still sets the strategic direction but challenges them to determine the best tactics for executing the strategy. If a salesperson is far enough along the Growth Curve that he is beginning to burn out, the manager can get him involved in learning more about the business of healthcare and show him what a strategic business call looks like. These prospective Phase III sales professionals need to see the personal and professional value that can come from having business dialogues with customers.

With Phase III people, the manager should focus on helping them tighten their strategic plans, challenge them to show what they know of their customers' critical success factors and organizational strategy and explain persuasively how their strategies link to these needs. For example, these sales reps might be asked to present a paper to the sales team that captures a current and relevant healthcare business issue, and then to show how the team members can use the information to develop strategy.

The manager always should be the ultimate strategist. He or she must be able to assess the current strengths and weaknesses of the team while being knowledgeable about competitors and the terrain. The strategic manager is able to direct the strategic and tactical activities of the team regardless of the individual members' levels of strategic understanding. A Phase III manager might also use team members' terrain knowledge to direct the strategies of the Phase I and II salespeople. This is valuable both because of the Phase III person's more detailed knowledge of the business terrain, and because it helps develop everyone's skills.

A key point here is that, in order to direct successful strategic efforts, someone on the team must be thoroughly informed concerning "self, other, and terrain." A good leader will use the appropriate skills to ensure that the strategy for each account is built on a firm foundation of relevant information.

Chapter Sixteen Summary

Understanding the different types of terrain is critical for determining strategy and for gaining a position of strength.

If you must go around someone blocking your progress in an account, try to unseat your competition completely and then rebuild the customer relationship. To avoid going around users, position yourself as a solution only where your competition is weak and also be able to connect your solution to a higher level Critical Success Factor or Strategy of the customer organization.

First mover position is ideal and gains you the high ground. If your competition has the high ground, use flanking tactics to display them and then move cautiously.

Managers must identify where their reps are on the Growth Curve and develop their teams accordingly to move them towards becoming Phase III strategists.

Knowledge is key to developing strategy.

Phase III strategists may sometimes choose to sustain a long-term customer relationship and ignore mandates by the home office in order to get longer-term gain and preserve a key relationship. Customers will appreciate the service and integrity of Phase III reps and find them new sales opportunities.

Individuals are often reluctant to do the work needed to move from Phase II to Phase III. Managers must earn the respect and dedication of these individuals by setting and sticking to firm expectations. Managers must determine the individual motivations of those on the sales team and direct the strategic and tactical actions of their sales professionals.

CHAPTER 17

Navigating Variations in Terrain

Sun Tzu said: The art of war recognizes nine varieties of ground:
(1) Dispersive ground;
(2) Facile ground;
(3) Contentious ground;
(4) Open ground;
(5) Ground of intersecting highways;
(6) Serious ground;
(7) Difficult ground;
(8) Hemmed-in ground;
(9) Desperate ground.

*W*hen a chieftain is fighting in his own territory, it is dispersive ground. When he has penetrated into hostile territory, but to no great distance, it is facile ground.

When we are well received within a customer's organization, we are able to move about with few restraints. Having this advantage is significant because it shows that we have gained a high level of credibility and trust with the customer. There are situations in which key account managers have even been given office space to use while they are working with the client. This gives representatives a great advantage because they are more likely to learn about the politics of the organization by working on site. They also will have greater acceptance at higher levels of influence within the account, and thus are able to learn more about the terrain issues. They will know when a competitor is trying to flank them.

Facile ground is analogous to a situation where a Phase III sales professional is able to move around in the account gathering information and positioning herself to pick off a piece of the competitor's business before he even knows that she was there.

Ground the possession of which imports great advantage to either side, is contentious ground.

Sun Tzu refers here to a situation where everyone is on an equal footing in the account and no one has the high ground with respect to market share or product positioning. An example might be a group purchasing organization that decides there will be a dual award of contracts to two competitors. Since there are only two of you, it is obvious where you must gather your competitive knowledge. Success in this instance might depend on who has the better pull-through strategy—a Phase III sales professional might say, you want the award to be dual, so I want to have 95% of the purchases and the competitor can have 5 percent. Since there are only two of you, you know upon whom you must focus your competitive knowledge.

Ground on which each side has liberty of movement is open ground.

When the customer is flexible enough to wait to see which competitor is the best strategic player, the situation is one of "open ground." Whoever develops, communicates, and executes the best strategy wins the business.

Ground which forms the key to three contiguous states, so that he who occupies it first has most of the Empire at his command, is a ground of intersecting highways.

If you are able to discover that one account's decision can affect several other accounts, this is a real coup. We once worked with an organization that was trying and failing to get their product on a hospital's formulary. After months of effort, the salesperson found out that this particular account was influenced by an individual who was not an early adopter of new products. The salesperson also found out that this influencer had a close friend who was in the same position in another hospital, but who was willing to move earlier to accept new products. If this early adopter felt the product was advantageous, he spoke to his more conservative friend and a change would happen.

Since the early adopter was not in this salesperson's territory, he was missing an opportunity to leverage success in that account to his own hospital. After meeting with the representative covering the other account, the two representatives developed a successful strategy to convert the slower hospital by first converting the early adopter.

Another example of "intersecting highways" is a national account strategy that uses contracts as leverage at the local account level. Winning these key accounts is very fortunate, but for those who are unable to influence the national account in favor of their local customer, they can also be frustrating. This is one reason why national account specialists should not develop their strategies in isolation from their local account colleagues.

When an army has penetrated into the heart of a hostile country, leaving a number of fortified cities in its rear, it is serious ground.

When you have only one position within an account and you are surrounded by a competitor in other areas of the account you must move quickly to establish more positions. Unless you leverage your initial position and grow as rapidly as possible, or your product may be viewed as out of place in the account. A good competitor will move quickly to either isolate you in that one position or move you out altogether.

An example of this might be an antibiotic that is added to the formulary in a hospital because it enjoys a singular advantage in a rare indication. You may want to expand your usage to other appropriate areas, but you have flanked to the rare indication because there are few, if any, competitors staking out that area. What a good competitor will do is to try to get you restricted to the single indication in order to protect their own business. A strategist uses success in the rare indication to move into more competitive — but still appropriate — indications. We have, in effect, left the "fortified city" behind so that we can at least get the product available for use.

Although winning a toehold in such a situation is an appropriate strategic move, you cannot stay in this one place for too long unless your objective is to maintain only that position. If the single position *is* indeed your objective, it may be worthwhile to form some sort of alliance with your competitors so that they realize you are not there to try to displace them. They may even be willing to assist you in your efforts to identify potential customers for your product for that one indication. We have seen situations where purchasing decisions are made for one item because the hospital uses more of a company's other offerings than those of an alternative product line. Individual physicians, however, may prefer the alternative products. Local buying consortia are constantly working on ways they can impact what they call PPIs or "physician preferred items." Should that occur, other buying criteria are certain to enter into the equation.

Mountain forests, rugged steeps, marshes and fens — all country that is hard to traverse: this is difficult ground.

Have you ever won business and then after the victory you wondered why you even bothered because the customer is so difficult? You must evaluate your resources against customer demands to determine if winning the account is worth the resulting extra work you must perform to sustain your product's use by that customer.

Ground which is reached through narrow gorges, and from which we can only retire by tortuous paths, so that a small number of the competitor would suffice to crush a large body of our men: this is hemmed-in ground.

Remember the first time you encountered that competitor who had been in the territory for most of his life? What a difficult situation that can be. Regardless of how much support you got or how many resources you had available to you for the opportunity, the customer simply did not want to harm the relationship they enjoyed with your competitor. Such an account can be extraordinarily difficult to penetrate if you take the usual route.

Your only opportunity to win here may be to find influencers in the account with which the competitor enjoys no relationship advantage. If the competitor is a Phase II representative, winning business may just be a matter of going into the account at a higher level and beginning your advance there. As we have said before, Phase III sales professionals usually approach a new account in this way. They want to reach the highest levels for two very important reasons:

- They need to get a clear picture of the critical success factors of the organization, and

- They want to avoid their Phase II competitors who are enjoying strong relationships at the lower levels in the account.

Gaining access continues to be a critical objective for getting a foot in the door in difficult account situations.

Ground, on which we can only be saved from destruction by fighting without delay, is desperate ground.

No salesperson really enjoys having to go in toward the end of the year to try to close an opportunity out of desperation. Minimize the odds of ending up in this situation by being consistently strategic throughout the year.

On dispersive ground, therefore, fight not. On facile ground, halt not. On contentious ground, attack not. On open ground, do not try to block the competitor's way. On the ground of intersecting highways, join hands with your allies. On serious ground, gather in plunder. In difficult ground, keep steadily on the march. On hemmed-in ground, resort to stratagem. On desperate ground, fight.

Those who were called skillful leaders of old knew how to drive a wedge between the competitor's front and rear; to prevent co-operation between his large and small divisions; to hinder the good troops from rescuing the bad, the officers from rallying their men

.

When the competitor's men were united, they managed to keep them in disorder. When it was to their advantage, they made a forward move; when otherwise, they stopped still.

A good strategist is able to keep her competitors off balance by being deliberate and cunning in how she communicates and executes her product positioning. She realizes that the competition will soon have the sales aids her company distributes, so she makes sure she is consciously using those aids to support her strategy. The Phase III sales professional can stay on-strategy in an account, while allowing her tactical execution to vary from one influencer to another. This makes it difficult for a competitor to take the product materials and ascertain what the strategic message actually is.

If you are able to keep the competitor guessing, he will find it difficult to rally his troops and resources to fight against you.

If asked how to cope with a great host of the competitor in orderly array and on the point of marching to the attack, I should say: "Begin by seizing something which your opponent holds dear; then he will be amenable to your will."

Rapidity is the essence of war: take advantage of the competitor's unreadiness, make your way by unexpected routes, and attack unguarded spots.

Ask yourself: When you focus your initial efforts around winning an account that is a strong supporter of your competitor, how powerfully do you make your initial statement? Establish a position, no matter how small, and your competitor will begin to work from a position of desperation and his efforts will show this. Plan your strategies well and flank your competitor quickly and efficiently and soon you will have a position of strength from which to leverage this success.

The following are the principles to be observed by an invading force: The further you penetrate into a country, the greater will be the solidarity of your troops, and thus the defenders will not prevail against you.

Make forays in fertile country in order to supply your army with food. Carefully study the well being of your men, and do not overtax them. Concentrate your energy and hoard your strength. Keep your army continually on the move, and devise unfathomable plans.

Success breeds success. Sharing upbeat account stories with the rest of the team can be highly motivational. As a manager and leader, reward your team once they begin to enjoy success and they will see the benefits of winning and winning quickly.

Once the successes start to multiply, revisit them and look for ways you can leverage the wins with other customers. "Concentrate your energy" on those things that are effective; make a note of ineffective tactics that should be avoided in the future.

Remember, though, that you must only celebrate successes for a short time. You need to immediately move on to growing and protecting business you have won because your competitors will surely be preparing to attack you.

Throw your soldiers into positions whence there is no escape, and they will prefer death to flight. If they will face death, there is nothing they may not achieve. Officers and men alike will put forth their uttermost strength.

Soldiers when in desperate straits lose the sense of fear. If there is no place of refuge, they will stand firm. If they are in hostile country, they will show a stubborn front. If there is no help for it, they will fight hard.

Thus, without waiting to be marshaled, the soldiers will be constantly on the qui vive; without waiting to be asked, they will do your will; without restrictions, they will be faithful; without giving orders, they can be trusted

Prohibit the taking of omens, and do away with superstitious doubts. Then, until death itself comes, no calamity need be feared.

If our soldiers are not overburdened with money, it is not because they have distaste for riches; if their lives are not unduly long, it is not because they are disinclined to longevity.

On the day they are ordered out to battle, your soldiers may weep, those sitting up bedewing their garments, and those lying down letting the tears run down their cheeks. But let them once be brought to bay, and they will display the courage of a Chu or a Kuei.

Desperation is not fun. Though desperation can lead to heroics in battle, in sales it tends to lead to burnout. It can also lead to desertion. When sales professionals feel there is no way they can achieve their objectives, they may decide to move on to another organization.

One especially powerful way managers can create an atmosphere of success is to involve salespeople in setting sales objectives and then committing to meeting them.

Tom Stovall recalls a situation in his career that illustrates this point:

"As a part of my professional development, the pharma company I was working for at the time gave me a field management position. I knew that this was to be a one- to two-year commitment designed to help me understand how to lead and manage field salespeople. Thus, I was given one of the lowest-performing divisions in the company."

"Almost immediately after moving my family to our new locale, I received the sales numbers for the division. Knowing their weak past performance, I decided to take a different approach with the team than had been used previously. In the past, each salesperson was given a sales objective for each product. This tended to be top-down, with the division manager pretty much just divvying up the division objectives among the members of the team."

"I decided I would change the game by meeting with each salesperson, going over the previous year's sales numbers, and asking him or her to come back to me with the number to which they would commit. This served several purposes. I would make sure each member knew how to read their sales reports and they would be making a personal and supported commitment to their sales growth. At the same time, I tried to come up with how I thought the sales might pan out for the team by looking at past results and at the numbers that had been handed me by my regional manager."

"It turned out that the numbers I had been given were irrelevant. After meeting with each salesperson, I saw that the team had come up with objectives that exceeded the regional manager's figures. I did need to push back on a couple of people, but that turned out to be because they didn't really understand the forecasting process. I clarified it for them and asked them to come back with a better projection of what they could contribute, which they did."

"Each month the team members were able to track their progress, and we could either celebrate success or make tactical or resource adjustments to help those who were trailing. There would be no surprises at the end of the year. With a few exceptions, everyone blasted through their numbers. We moved from the lowest-performing division into the top 10 in all products."

"This was a real learning experience for me. I found that when good people make a commitment, they will do everything they can to deliver on their commitment. They just need the support of their managers and, on occasion, firm guidance as well as SMART objectives."

The skillful tactician may be likened to the shuai-jan. Now the shuai-jan is a snake that is found in the Chung Mountains. Strike at its head, and you will be attacked by its tail; strike at its tail, and you will be attacked by its head; strike at its middle, and you will be attacked by head and tail both.

Asked if an army can be made to imitate the shuai-jan, I should answer, Yes. For the men of Wu and the men of Yueh are enemies; yet if they are crossing a river in the same boat and are caught by a storm, they will come to each other's assistance just as the left hand helps the right.

Hence it is not enough to put one's trust in the tethering of horses, and the burying of chariot wheels in the ground.

The principle on which to manage an army is to set up one standard of courage which all must reach. How to make the best of both strong and weak—that is a question involving the proper use of ground. Thus the skillful general conducts his army just as though he were leading a single man, willy-nilly, by the hand.

In order to achieve the greatest possible success, a good leader and manager must know the talents and skills of his or her people and put the team members into situations where they will shine. In other words, you need the ability to identify the personal strategies of your people and to put those strategies to work toward achieving organizational objectives.

Personal strategies are based on the talents — the innate capabilities — that individuals possess. If individuals know their talents, they need to communicate these to their managers. If they don't know their talents, the manager should consider conducting an assessment to help identify them. (*Now, Discover Your Strengths*, by Marcus Buckingham, is an excellent resource.)

Once a manager knows the strengths and weaknesses of team members, the manager should try to put each individual into situations in which they can exercise their talents to achieve their objectives and those of their team. When individuals are able to exercise their own talents, they will be much more fulfilled and empowered.

It is the business of a general to be quiet and thus ensure secrecy; upright and just, and thus maintain order. He must be able to mystify his officers and men by false reports and appearances, and thus keep them in total ignorance.

By altering his arrangements and changing his plans, he keeps the competitor without definite knowledge. By shifting his camp and taking circuitous routes, he prevents the competitor from anticipating his purpose.

At the critical moment, the leader of an army acts like one who has climbed up a height and then kicks away the ladder behind him. He carries his men deep into hostile territory before he shows his hand.

He burns his boats and breaks his cooking-pots; like a shepherd driving a flock of sheep, he drives his men this way and that, and no one knows whither he is going.

To muster his host and bring it into danger: this may be termed the business of the general.

A strategic leader and manager must be cautious about communicating strategy. He or she needs to realize that when strategy is shared with a large number of people, it is likely that the strategy will become known to the competition in short order. So, be cautious with whom you share your strategy.

In some large accounts with multiple individuals working on tactical support, however, you *will* need to communicate your strategy because many of those same individuals may have worked with you on developing that strategy. Be as certain as possible, however, with regard to the intent of your team member before delivering that strategic information.

When a new product is about to be launched, sales and marketing leadership should be very careful about communicating strategy until the product is available for customers to use. If the strategy is communicated too early, competitors will be able to initiate blocking maneuvers that will create complications upon release of the product.

As we have seen, deception in the form of discretion can be important in the period prior to the product launch. For example, promotional materials might provide only general information on the product and nothing that gives away the winnable positions we will be using. Competitors will begin to attack and position themselves in any number of ways that will become irrelevant when the actual strategy is revealed.

At the field and account level there is also value in being discrete. Phase III sales professionals are careful about to whom they communicate their account strategy beyond the colleagues who are involved in the effort. At the same time, they ensure that anyone who enters the account is given the appropriate amount of strategic and tactical direction.

The months just prior to launch are the ideal time for learning the terrain and uncovering potential account strategies so that when the product is released, you can unleash powerful strategic advantage.

The different measures suited to the nine varieties of ground, the expediency of aggressive or defensive tactics, and the fundamental laws of human nature: these are things that must most certainly be studied.

When invading hostile territory, the general principle is, that penetrating deeply brings cohesion; penetrating but a short way means dispersion.

When you leave your own country behind, and take your army across neighboring territory, you find yourself on critical ground. When there are means of communication on all four sides, the ground is one of intersecting highways.

When you penetrate deeply into a country, it is serious ground. When you penetrate but a little way, it is facile ground.

When you have the competitor's strongholds on your rear, and narrow passes in front, it is hemmed-in ground.

When there is no place of refuge at all, it is desperate ground.

Therefore, on dispersive ground, I would inspire my men with unity of purpose. On facile ground, I would see that there is close connection between all parts of my army. On contentious ground, I would hurry up my rear. On open ground, I would keep a vigilant eye on my defenses. On ground of intersecting highways, I would consolidate my alliances. On serious ground, I would try to ensure a continuous stream of supplies. On difficult ground, I would keep pushing on along the road. On hemmed-in ground, I would block any way of retreat. On desperate ground, I would proclaim to my soldiers the hopelessness of saving their lives.

For it is the soldier's disposition to offer an obstinate resistance when surrounded, to fight hard when he cannot help himself, and to obey promptly when he has fallen into danger.
We cannot enter into alliance with neighboring princes until we are acquainted with their designs.

We are not fit to lead an army on the march unless we are familiar with the face of the country — its mountains and forests, its pitfalls and precipices, its marshes and swamps.
We shall be unable to turn natural advantages to account unless we make use of local guides.

In order to develop and execute a successful strategic position, we must have a thorough understanding of the terrain. Sun Tzu's direction here is highly relevant to developing competitive strategies in sales and marketing.

The obvious terrain knowledge that everyone on the team must have includes:

- Who the decision makers are and how they can be accessed.

- What decision-making process the customer uses.

- Who is on the Pharmacy and Therapeutics Committee or other such approval committee?

• Who your key competitor is and who supports them in the account.

The Phase III strategic individual will also know two other key pieces of information:

• What the account's strategy is.

• What the critical success factors are for the influencers at all levels in the account.

Of course you are likely to encounter many competitors in an account, so you will need to find"insider resources"—what Sun Tzu calls"local guides"—to help you navigate the difficult political and competitive terrain issues. In your accounts, these will be the individuals who help you approach the opportunity without stepping on any landmines.

Case Study: Using Local Guides

Lily, a sales professional was challenged to position her antibiotic on the formulary in one of her key hospitals. The Pharmacy Director, Rex, was not interested in adding the antibiotic since he felt that the pathogens were already well covered and he anticipated that the new antibiotic would be a significant drain on the pharmacy budget.

Lily was upset by Rex's stance because she felt that her antibiotic, though more expensive per dose, might actually be less expensive since it could be dosed less frequently than her competitor's. She needed to talk with someone who had the power to help with the pharmacy budget issue.

Through her relationship with the Director of Nursing, Lily found out that an effort was underway by the service line managers to decrease length of stay at the hospital. Lily asked the Nursing Director if she could introduce her to one of the service line managers so that she could learn more about their responsibilities within the hospital.

Lily's first call was a strategic business call on the Cardiac Service Line Manager, Donna. During the call, Lily learned more about Donna's responsibilities, her reporting structure, and, most importantly, what her critical success factors were for the coming year. Shortening length of stay was at the top of the list. Lily asked Donna if she could suggest another contact within the hospital from whom Lily might gain another perspective on the same issues. Donna suggested the Clinical Pharmacist, Lauren.

Lily had met with Lauren in the past, but mainly to deliver her technical product information or to arrange for other product presentations of a purely clinical nature. This time, her objective was to uncover Lauren's critical success factors. With the context gained from her discussion with the Donna, Lily was able to learn about Pharmacy's perspective on length of stay issues.

After a few more strategic business calls, Lily returned to Donna, her "local guide," to report her findings. Lily's strategy with her antibiotic: Potential Impact on Length of Stay.

Positioning her product as a way of helping meet the goal of reducing length of stay, while also strengthening quality was a compelling strategy. Lily's tactics supported that strategy. Donna, in coordination with Lauren, saw to it that Pharmacy and Therapeutics Committee heard the story.

Lily was successful, but what about Rex, the Director of Pharmacy? Once Lily's product was being used, she met with Donna and Lauren to see if her product had delivered both in terms of clinical needs and of helping bring length of stay down. The answer was yes on both counts.

Armed with this positive response, Lily prepared a half-page letter addressed to the Chief of Operations (Rex's boss) and copied to the VP of Medical Management (Donna's boss), the CFO, Lauren, Donna, and Rex. The letter read something like this:

"For the past several weeks I have had the opportunity to meet with several individuals around the hospital. My objective has been to gain a broader understanding of the issues and challenges you are facing in the hospital.

"One key initiative I have learned about is your effort to decrease length of stay while positively affecting quality. It has been a pleasure to work with Donna, Lauren, and Rex to ensure that we are providing products and services which are positively affecting quality and length of stay. My commitment to you is to continue to look for ways that we can provide value addressing both clinical and professional objectives. My card is enclosed. If I can be of any assistance to you, please don't hesitate to contact me directly or through Rex."

Upper management spoke very favorably of the letter to Rex and the other members of the LOS team. Lily got a warm reception from Rex the next time she called on him. Imagine the competitive advantage she had gained by taking the important step of enlisting a local guide in her sales effort. This understanding of the terrain, strategic focus on uncovered Critical Success Factors, and expert execution of tactical tools before and after the product was used helped Lily to build her competitive immunity.

Local guides may also be individuals who have been hired in your organization and who once were employed by your competition. Seek them out for their valuable insights.

Beyond the obvious benefit of this type of insider information to the individual who has the account responsibility, it is also critical that this information be communicated to others within your organization that may be assisting with the account. If you do not pass terrain information along, not only are you likely to suffer negative consequences, but you will also forego the synergy that can make a difference in achieving your objectives in the account. And if this terrain information isn't passed along to sales and marketing management, the organization will be unable to leverage your fine work as a "Rapid Expeditionary Force" member.

When you are attempting to penetrate an account, making use of local guides will help you flank your competitor with your solution. If you already hold the high ground within an account, you can use local guides to help you enhance your relationships and build your competitive immunity, thus keeping your competitors from flanking you.

To be ignorant of any one of the following four or five principles does not befit a warlike prince. When a warlike prince attacks a powerful state, his generalship shows itself in preventing the concentration of the competitor's forces. He overawes his opponents, and their allies are prevented from joining against him.

Hence he does not strive to ally himself with all and sundry, nor does he foster the power of other states. He carries out his own secret designs, keeping his antagonists in awe. Thus he is able to capture their cities and overthrow their kingdoms.

A Phase III, strategic, consultative sales professional keeps her strategies to herself and allows insights into her plan only to a select few. In this way she is able to keep her competitors guessing as to what her approach might be. She will have different strategies for different accounts so her competitors are unable to discern any consistency in her message. For these reasons, her competitors must protect themselves on all flanks, which prevents them from focusing on their own differentiating advantages.

Bestow rewards without regard to rule, issue orders without regard to previous arrangements, and you will be able to handle a whole army as though you had to do with but a single man.

Confront your soldiers with the deed itself; never let them know your design. When the outlook is bright, bring it before their eyes; but tell them nothing when the situation is gloomy.

Place your army in deadly peril, and it will survive; plunge it into desperate straits, and it will come off in safety.

For it is precisely when a force has fallen into harm's way that is capable of striking a blow for victory.

Success in warfare is gained by carefully accommodating ourselves to the competitor's purpose.

By persistently hanging on the competitor's flank, we shall succeed in the long run in killing the commander-in-chief. This is called ability to accomplish a thing by sheer cunning.

On the day that you take up your command, block the frontier passes, destroy the official tallies, and stop the passage of all emissaries. Be stern in the council-chamber, so that you may control the situation.

Once a Phase III sales professional assumes responsibility for an account, he should be the lead strategist, directing the efforts of all other team members that have account involvement. The sales professional leading on the account should work closely with his manager, with whom he needs to have an open and trusting relationship. If this relationship is strained, success may be limited.

If the competitor leaves a door open, you must rush in. Forestall your opponent by seizing what he holds dear, and subtly contrive to time his arrival on the ground.
Walk in the path defined by rule, and accommodate yourself to the competitor until you can fight a decisive battle.

At first, then, exhibit the coyness of a maiden, until the competitor gives you an opening; afterwards emulate the rapidity of a running hare, and it will be too late for the competitor to oppose you.

Your competitors will have their supporters, too. If we are going to be successful in displacing a competitor who already enjoys the "high ground" in an account, we must flank them. This involves two critical steps: gaining access to other levels of influence in the organization and finding an aspect of their solution that is weak and positioning our strength against that weakness. We don't ask a customer to cease using the competitive product; obviously, they chose the competitor's solution based on the best information they had at the time. To ask them to switch over completely would probably meet with counterproductive pushback. We simply ask them to consider using our product as a solution for that one weak area.

To discover a universally agreed-upon competitive weakness and, customer critical success factors/strategies, we must do our homework. Once we uncover this information, we must make our approach quick and decisive to connect our solution to the area of weakness and to the customer's critical success factors and strategy, which we have uncovered through strategic business calls.

Chapter Seventeen Summary

It is important to identify variations in terrain and know how to adapt your strategy to navigate each one:

- Accessible terrain gives us great advantages in being able to flank out competitors without their knowing.

- Equal footing limits the competitive knowledge you need to have and requires you be creative in meeting the terms of the agreement to push it to your advantage.

- Open ground requires you to develop communication and execute strategy better than your competition.

- Finding intersections between account influencers can be extremely useful terrain information to have.

Begin by gaining a small toehold via your product's main strengths. Follow up on this with a more focused strategy for gaining additional market share.

Assess your customers to ensure their demands after you win the account will not overload your resources.

When cornered, find influencers with whom the competition has no relationship in the account and gain access through them.

Be consistently strategic to avoid year-end, desperate situations.

Communicate your product positioning carefully and vary your tactical execution by client so you competition will be unable to determine what your strategy is.

Establish a position in an account—no matter how small your competition will have to work to defend their own.

Leverage wins with customers by seeing what you can apply to other accounts.

Involve your sales professionals in setting and committing to sales goals.

Know what terrain knowledge you must have in order to execute strategy effectively. Use local guides to navigate difficult areas of the account.

CHAPTER 18

Attack by Fire

Sun Tzu said: There are five ways of attacking with fire. The first is to burn soldiers in their camp; the second is to burn stores; the third is to burn baggage trains; the fourth is to burn arsenals and magazines; the fifth is to hurl dropping fire amongst the competitor.

I n order to carry out an attack, we must have means available. The material for raising fire should always be kept in readiness.

There is a proper season for making attacks with fire, and special days for starting a conflagration.

The proper season is when the weather is very dry; the special days are those when the moon is in the constellations of the Sieve, the Wall, the Wing or the Crossbar; for these four are all days of rising wind.

In attacking with fire, one should be prepared to meet five possible developments:

(1) When fire breaks out inside the competitor's camp, respond at once with an attack from without.

(2) If there is an outbreak of fire, but the competitor's soldiers remain quiet, bide your time and do not attack.

(3) When the force of the flames has reached its height, follow it up with an attack, if that is practicable; if not, stay where you are.

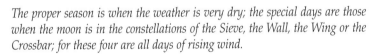

(4) If it is possible to make an assault with fire from without, do not wait for it to break out within, but deliver your attack at a favorable moment.

(5) When you start a fire, be to windward of it. Do not attack from the leeward.

A wind that rises in the daytime lasts long, but a night breeze soon falls. In every army, the five developments connected with fire must be known, the movements of the stars calculated, and a watch kept for the proper days.

Hence those who use fire as an aid to the attack show intelligence; those who use water as an aid to the attack gain an accession of strength. By means of water, a competitor may be intercepted, but not robbed of all his belongings.

In our sales and marketing interpretation of Sun Tzu, "using fire" means that you have decided to take a chance in a competitive situation, which might result in ruining relationships in the account. There are situations where we have seen this done with a positive outcome. An example is the case study at the beginning of Chapter One. The sales rep in this case gathered key Critical Success Factor information from a variety of individuals in the account, risking that his customer would resent his going above him to talk about issues and solutions. Fortunately, the rep gathered information that allowed him to present a creative solution that addressed the customer's issues and outweighed the negative repercussions around where the rep gathered the needed information.

We have heard horror stories of "fire" assaults that won business at the cost of ruined relationships that were never repaired. For example, we once spoke with the CEO of a large integrated health system about supplier organizations that had excelled and those that had, in his judgment, failed his organization. He told us the story of a company that had lost a contract in his laboratory.

The CEO described how, several weeks after the contract was awarded, a high-level executive from one of the companies that had lost the bid contacted him for a short meeting. After a brief introduction, the company representatives at the meeting told him, in effect, that one of his lab directors had made a foolish mistake by going with a competitor for their lab contract. The CEO said that the gist of the meeting was the losing company's effort to stop the contract from moving forward. He told them that the decision had been made, and they finally left.

The lab director who had been criticized was a personal friend of the CEO, and she had the respect of everyone in the organization. The CEO said that he picked up the phone and called her to let her know that the competitive company had just left a meeting with him during which they told him how foolish she was in making her decision. The CEO said that they laughed about it for a couple of minutes, but he also said that he wanted her to know what was being said so that she would be aware of the competitive company's tactics.

Needless to say, the lab director was not laughing about it once she hung up the phone. When we spoke with her later, she told us how insulting she found the competitive company's approach. Their salesperson got an icy reception at his next appointment, and the relationship between this lab director and the company still suffers after many years.

"Setting fires" can have strong effects both positively and negatively. As a strategist, you need to decide when such a tactic is called for. If used inappropriately, it can cause damage from which you may never recover. But when applied appropriately, it can turn zero sales into significant success.

Unhappy is the fate of one who tries to win his battles and succeed in his attacks without cultivating the spirit of enterprise; for the result is waste of time and general stagnation.
Hence the saying: The enlightened ruler lays his plans well ahead; the good general cultivates his resources.

Move not unless you see an advantage; use not your troops unless there is something to be gained; fight not unless the position is critical. No ruler should put troops into the field merely to gratify his own spleen; no general should fight a battle simply out of pique.

If it is to your advantage, make a forward move; if not, stay where you are.

Anger may in time change to gladness; vexation may be succeeded by content. But a kingdom that has once been destroyed can never come again into being; nor can the dead ever be brought back to life.

Hence the enlightened ruler is heedful, and the good general full of caution. This is the way to keep a country at peace and an army intact.

A successful strategist leading a sales team must know when to make a competitive move and when to hold the current position. This means you have analyzed self, other, and terrain, as well as considering what your competitor's responses to your move might be. By involving the sales team in this process, you will be able to consolidate everyone's terrain insights and local guide information concerning how the competitor is likely to attack or defend, and what all this might mean to strategic positioning and tactical execution.

By then considering the "nightmare scenario" for the opportunity you can be sure you come up with a strategy and tactics that are likely to stand against competitive attacks and to questions from your customers.

By insisting that the strategic homework be completed prior to moving your sales team toward execution, you will be much more likely to succeed. Since planning is treated as a prerequisite to successful strategy, your team will learn that they will not be expected to throw themselves into an effort that is futile, and they will be more likely to exceed your expectations.

A strategist must try to act objectively and practically. Sun Tzu warns against making moves based on emotion, since this will usually result in tactical sloppiness due to lack of strategic direction.

Chapter Eighteen Summary

"Attack by fire" is a serious tactic to be used only in select situations. It has the risk of ruining relationships and must be used carefully, although when used appropriately it can increase sales.

Insist that strategic homework is completed prior to developing strategy and implementing tactics—never make moves based on emotion.

CHAPTER 19

The Use of Spies

Sun Tzu said: Raising a host of a hundred thousand men and marching them great distances entails heavy loss on the people and a drain on the resources of the State. The daily expenditure will amount to a thousand ounces of silver. There will be commotion at home and abroad, and men will drop down exhausted on the highways. As many as seven hundred thousand families will be impeded in their labor.

W hen at all possible, keep your sales team close to home. Especially with the most critical customers, it is important that the account managers be highly accessible. When needs and problems arise, customers want to have a salesperson who is easy to contact and able to come on-site at short notice. Customers also want to know that the salesperson is a direct link to the company they are buying from; the salesperson needs to be the "go-to" person for the account. This is difficult to achieve when sales territories are too large, either in terms of geographic coverage, or in terms of the number of accounts each sales professional handles.

Hostile armies may face each other for years, striving for the victory which is decided in a single day. This being so, to remain in ignorance of the competitor's condition simply because one grudges the outlay of a hundred ounces of silver in honors and emoluments, is the height of inhumanity.

One who acts thus is no leader of men, no present help to his sovereign, no master of victory.

Thus, what enables the wise sovereign and the good general to strike and conquer, and achieve things beyond the reach of ordinary men, is foreknowledge.

Now this foreknowledge cannot be elicited from spirits; it cannot be obtained inductively from experience, or by any deductive calculation.

Knowledge of the competitor's dispositions can only be obtained from other men.

Our ability to develop relevant strategies based on timely information is vital to success. Technology and purchased sales and competitive data can make us lazy—knowing that our competitors have the same purchased data available to them can motivate us to gather critical terrain information ourselves.

Sales and marketing departments must ensure that they have both identified their Phase III sales professionals and that they have won these individuals' trust so that honest communication can happen. In the military, the Special Forces troops are the ones who go into the field of battle first in order to provide communications and to pass along terrain data to the appropriate people at headquarters. Phase III sales professionals are the "special forces" terrain experts for the sales and marketing organization. While relevant information of any kind is important, the account-specific information that comes from your Phase III field personnel can spell the difference between success or failure for your products.

Sun Tzu refers to such special forces as his "spies." For us, the spy can be thought of as the "informer" within the account (some refer to him or her as the "coach" within the account), the Phase III account manager himself or herself, or a new-hire who has had experience working either in the account or with a key competitor.

Sun Tzu also tells us that we need to test the information we gain, whether from an internal or external source, in order to ensure that it is accurate and to determine how complete it is.

Hence the use of spies, of whom there are five classes: (1) Local spies; (2) inward spies; (3) converted spies; (4) doomed spies; (5) surviving spies.

When these five kinds of spy are all at work, none can discover the secret system. This is called "divine manipulation of the threads." It is the sovereign's most precious faculty. Having local spies means employing the services of the inhabitants of a district. Having inward spies, making use of officials of the competitor.

Having converted spies, getting hold of the competitor's spies and using them for our own purposes.

Having doomed spies, doing certain things openly for purposes of deception, and allowing our spies to know of them and report them to the competitor.

Surviving spies, finally, are those who bring back news from the competitor's camp.

Hence it is that which none in the whole army are more intimate relations to be maintained than with spies. None should be more liberally rewarded. In no other business should greater secrecy be preserved.

Spies cannot be usefully employed without a certain intuitive sagacity. They cannot be properly managed without benevolence and straightforwardness. Without subtle ingenuity of mind, one cannot make certain of the truth of their reports.

Be subtle. And use your spies for every kind of business. If a secret piece of news is divulged by a spy before the time is ripe, he must be put to death together with the man to whom the secret was told.

Whether the object be to crush an army, to storm a city, or to assassinate an individual, it is always necessary to begin by finding out the names of the attendants, the aides-de-camp, and door-keepers and sentries of the general in command. Our spies must be commissioned to ascertain these.

The competitor's spies who have come to spy on us must be sought out, tempted with bribes, led away and comfortably housed. Thus they will become converted spies and available for our service.

It is through the information brought by the converted spy that we are able to acquire and employ local and inward spies. It is owing to his information, again, that we can cause the doomed spy to carry false tidings to the competitor.

Lastly, it is by his information that the surviving spy can be used on appointed occasions.

The end and aim of spying in all its five varieties is knowledge of the competitor; and this knowledge can only be derived, in the first instance, from the converted spy.

Hence it is essential that the converted spy be treated with the utmost liberality.

Of old, the rise of the Yin dynasty was due to Li Chih who had served under the Hsia. Likewise, the rise of the Chou dynasty was due to Lu Ya who had served under the Yin.

Hence it is only the enlightened ruler and the wise general who will use the highest intelligence of the army for purposes of spying and thereby they achieve great results. Spies are a most important element in water, because on them depends an army's ability to move.

Here Sun Tzu presents some harsh reality with regard to war—yet there is still some relevance to any kind of competitive scenario.

Your Phase III strategic, consultative sales and marketing professionals are the keys to the current and future success of your organization. This is especially true now that healthcare sales and marketing practices are under close scrutiny.

Your ability to identify and hire these Phase III strategists is, by itself, a difficult project. There are questions that may be asked when you are in the final stages such as:

- What is your personal strategy? A fall back question for this might be: What talent do you possess that you feel gives you a competitive advantage with regard to this position?

- What do you see as our organizational strategy?

- What are the 2-3 critical issues facing our customer base, today?

The Phase III approach is one of integrity, insight, commitment to the marketplace, and steady focus on solving issues for customers. The ability of Phase III sales professionals to integrate their organization's solutions with appropriate customer needs is what sets them apart from their more tactical peers and competitors. Because of their integrative skills, Phase III salespeople have ready access to customers.

Sun Tzu speaks often about "spies." In our world, they are individuals who either have great insight into the local terrain, our competitors, or people who have commonality with our customers — healthcare professionals — and thus strong relationships. These strengths lead to more focused solutions to customer problems. They also enable the individuals in question to gather local terrain information more rapidly than those who don't have in-depth terrain and healthcare experience. Look around your own organization for these people.

Chapter Nineteen Summary

Being accessible by your customers is a major strategic advantage. Keep this in mind when redeploying territories and carving geographic boundaries.

Today, access to data is easy but everyone, including your competitors, has the same data. Competitive advantage does not manifest in purchased data. You must continue to gather personal terrain information for all your key accounts.

Making use of spies within ethical bounds is highly advantageous.

Conclusion

"Tactics without strategy is the noise before defeat."

-Sun Tzu, *The Art of War*

Strategy is the most critical element to your success as a sales professional in today's healthcare marketplace. We hope that *Building Competitive Immunity* has shown you how to become strategic through acquiring critical, higher level knowledge—about yourself, your competition, and the overall healthcare and customer terrain.

The exercises you've completed in Chapters One through Five have pinpointed your strengths and weaknesses. We encourage you to return to these often for an ongoing evaluation of where you stand and how you can work on yourself to become and remain a relevant resource for your customers. Becoming this resource will give you increased access to both your current customers and to higher level influencers.

As you continue to add to your higher level of understanding, it will also be valuable to continually assess your customer relationships in the context of Sun Tzu's text, *The Art of War.* Your increased knowledge of strategy will afford you an ever-deeper understanding of Sun Tzu's advice, which you will find relevant to more and more sales situations. And the more strategic you become, the more successful you'll be at Building Competitive Immunity—for yourself and your company.

Please feel free to contact us with any questions you may have. We always welcome comments and feedback. You can reach us through www.sgbci.com.